☞ *THE BEST EXCUSE . . .*

THE BEST

 THE FINE ART

EXCUSE . . .

OF . . .

getting out of social engagements, domestic chores,

boring conversations, unwanted work, infidelity,

talking to salesmen, giving presents,

looking for jobs, eating inedibles,

paying bills, forgetting birthdays,

not showing up, and making

poor excuses

by

DONALD CARROLL

Coward-McCann, Inc., New York

Copyright © 1983 by Donald Carroll
All rights reserved.
This book, or parts thereof, may not be reproduced in any form
without permission in writing from the publisher.
Published on the same day in Canada by General Publishing Co. Limited, Toronto.

Library of Congress Cataloging in Publication Data

Carroll, Donald, date.
The best excuse . . .

Subtitle: The fine art of getting out of social
engagements, domestic chores, boring conversations,
unwanted work, infidelity, talking to salesmen, giving
presents, looking for jobs, eating inedibles, paying
bills, forgetting birthdays, not showing up, and making
poor excuses.
1. Excuses—Anecdotes, facetiae, satire, etc.
I. Title.
PN6231.E87C37   1983   818′.5402   82-18186
ISBN 0-698-11219-9

Designed by Helen Barrow

For Colman and Leslie

Contents

INTRODUCTION

*The Fine Art of
Making Excuses*

Before we begin considering the infinite beauty and utility of the well-made excuse, we must first address ourselves to an uncomfortable fact: Excuses have a bad name. *"Qui s'excuse, s'accuse,"* wrote the sixteenth-century Frenchman Gabriel Meurier. "He who excuses himself accuses himself." This attitude, sadly, is still with us.

Most people see excuses simply as lies in fancy dress. Thus when they "see through" an excuse they think their ability to incriminate a failed excuser derives from their ability to discriminate between what is true and what is not. In fact, of course, that discrimination cannot possibly be made with any degree of certainty. If it could, the only effective excuses would be absolutely truthful ones. And that, we know, is not the case.

It is well to remember, then, that excuses are merely the stated grounds for avoiding some future activity, or avoiding the consequences of some past activity. As such, they are morally neutral; it is the use to which they are put that invites moral scrutiny. The only value judgment one can make about an excuse per se is based on an exclusively functional criterion: Does it work? If it does, it's a good excuse. If it doesn't, it isn't.

Truthfulness, by which I mean adherence to a set of objectively verifiable facts, is quite irrelevant to the effectiveness of an excuse. If your excuse is unconvincing, you are as apt to get into trouble for telling the unvarnished truth as you are for concocting a monstrous falsehood. Indeed, you are *more* apt to get into trouble, because if you are telling the truth there is a good chance that the person you are trying to convince has heard it all before—he has probably even used the excuse himself—and therefore will tend to be unusually, and unfairly, skeptical.

So the truth should be treated just like any other element that goes into the making of an excuse: You should use only enough to make the excuse believable. If you inject too much pure truth—or pure fiction, for that matter—you risk killing the excuse by an overdose. It may well be that the truth in its unalloyed form provides you with a perfectly respectable justification for extricating yourself from an unwanted situation, but if it makes for a bad excuse it will do more harm than good.

Nor will the harm be restricted to your credibility. Excessive truthfulness can also have a damaging effect on the psychological well-being of those who are exposed to it. We often forget that excuses have a twofold function. Their primary function, of course, is to liberate us from circumstances we wish to escape. However, they also serve a valuable social purpose: By protecting innocent people from sudden and massive outbreaks of Truth, they help to minimize the number of civilian casualties we leave behind as we make our escape. This charitable aspect of excuse-making is best summed up in the great maxim handed down to us by generations of epistemologists: "What they don't know won't hurt them."

If you have any doubts about the nobility, not to mention the wisdom, of rationing the truth when fashioning an excuse, consider the following hypothetical situation: You are invited to a dinner party by a generous and well-meaning friend, but you are unable to attend. Now the *truth* is that you are unable to attend because you fear death by boredom when your friend gets drunk after dinner, as he inevitably does, and starts telling those tedious, repetitive, interminable stories of his, and besides, his wife's conversation is about as interesting as her cooking, the two of which combined would be enough to make one seek refuge in a sensory deprivation chamber, provided you didn't pass out first from the effects of having to talk to those cretins she surrounds herself with, though at least they take your mind off the nauseating wallpaper and the plastic upholstery and those hideous prints on the wall from the early Sears, Roebuck school of art that cry out to be defaced every time you see them. . . .

The *untruth*, on the other hand, involves nothing more complicated or wounding than a planned prior engagement, or perhaps an unplanned minor calamity, that will—what rotten luck—deny you the pleasure of their company.

Now ask yourself: Given a situation such as this, which excuse—the baldly truthful one or the cosmetically retouched one—is more likely to leave your friend with his ego intact? Which is more likely to preserve your friendship? Which is more likely to preserve Western civilization as we know it?

Exactly. So you need never feel any compunction about being creative when excusing yourself. The art of making excuses, after all, requires artistry.

As I have already indicated, there are two basic types of excuses. The first type comprises all those excuses designed to get you out of having to do something you consider unpleasant or unworthy of you. These are known as preemptive excuses, and they will be discussed in Part I of this book. The second type consists of those excuses designed to get you out of trouble for having done something that *others* consider unpleasant or unworthy of you. These are known as exculpatory excuses, and will be dealt with in Part II. They are also known, if they work, as "good reasons." If they don't work, they are called alibis.

Both types of excuses can be subdivided into six general categories: the familial, the financial, the medical, the meteorological, the technological, and the calendarial. A few words about each are in order.

THE FAMILIAL EXCUSE

The familial is really an umbrella category, a sort of holding company for other excuses, which can always be depended on to furnish you with a silent partner whenever one is needed to shore up another excuse. For example:

> *I can't understand why you haven't received it. I gave it to my son to mail over a week ago.*

> *I'll certainly be there. Let's see, what date is that? The 20th? Are you sure? Damn. That's my grandmother's birthday.*

> *Sounds like a super evening. You two always bring back such beautiful slides. Let me just check with John to see if he has anything planned.*

I'm completely stranded here. My daughter went off with the car keys.

I've been dying to hear all about your operation. Wait, hang on a second. I think I just heard a scream from the kids' room. Let me call you back.

That's strange. It's not like Mary to forget to give me a message.

I wish I could go with you, believe me, because that's the weekend my wife invited her mother to come and stay.

Of course I find you attractive. It's just that my father/mother/brother/sister/son/daughter/husband/wife might come home at any minute.

The great beauty of the familial category of excuses, as you will discover for yourself, is that the permutations and variations available within it are virtually endless. And the possibilities can be expanded even further by adopting, for excusatory purposes, an extended family—one that includes aunts, uncles, cousins, babysitters, the neighbors' kids, even ex-spouses. Another advantage of this type of excuse is that it takes the ball out of your court. Instantly the blame belongs to someone else, so you are exempt from any responsibility in the matter.

As versatile as the familial excuse is, there are two caveats that you should bear in mind. First, before taking on a silent partner in any given excuse, be certain that the partner will *remain* silent. This applies especially to children. You do not want to overhear your offspring saying to your boss, "Why would my father need to go with me to have my tonsils out? They were taken out two years ago!"

Second, when incorporating elderly family members into your excuses, beware of killing them off at a pace that exceeds their actual mortality rate. For one thing, your relatives are of more use to you alive than dead. For another thing, funerals have been used so often in the past to account for absences that they have only limited value anyway. And, finally, if you are seen to be bereaved more frequently than is normal, some churls might be tempted to start keeping a body count. Thus at some future date you could find yourself in the embarrassing position of being challenged when you claim to have been in the company of a beloved aunt whose funeral you attended several years and many excuses ago.

THE FINANCIAL EXCUSE

The financial excuse, which rests on your tactical insolvency, can range all the way down the circumstantial scale from the truly calamitous (your business has been wiped out; your personal debts are so monumental that you have been forced to declare bankruptcy) to the temporarily unsettling (you have a cash flow problem because your debtors are delinquent in their payments; you left your wallet in the taxi on the way to the restaurant) to the merely frustrating (you couldn't find anyone to make change for the pay telephone; you got caught without cash on a Sunday). In addition, spanning all these is a wonderful broad-spectrum excuse: *money worries*. You will be amazed at how many things you will be excused from, or excused for, because you have "money worries."

At the same time, you have to be selective in using financial excuses because some of the most popular are also too true to be good. For example, you must never try to get out of something on the grounds that you can't afford it. *Of course* you can't afford it, whatever "it" is. Nobody can. Therefore its affordability is beside the point. If people only spent money when they could afford to, we would still have a barter economy.

So if you are to succeed in selling someone a financial excuse, you had better be a strict monetarist. In other words, your problem is not that this or that is too expensive. Expensiveness, like affordability, is a vague, relative concept. Your problem is that you have *no cash*. That's a clear, absolute concept.

THE MEDICAL EXCUSE

Another tried-and-sometimes-true type of excuse is the medical one. In this category you have at your disposal all the ills that the flesh is heir to— an entire galaxy of allergies and phobias, diseases and viruses, ruptures and fractures, symptoms and diagnoses—from which to choose the affliction that best suits your purposes. For this very reason, however, it is important to choose an ailment that is appropriate to the occasion. Everyday aches and pains don't qualify. Indeed, any excuse that incorporates the word "ache" is likely to be considered highly suspect, because most of us tend to associate the word not with a specific pain but with a specific person who has used (or misused) the word in the past—someone who got a headache at the mention of sex, or a backache at the mention of a lawn mower, or a stomachache at the mention of okra, or an earache at the mention of homework.

But if familiarity with these complaints has bred contempt, the un-familiarity of others can work to your advantage. The same person who would react with a skeptical shrug to the news that you have a stomachache will panic at the news that you have possible trichinosis with concomitant nausea, facial edema, muscular encystment, blood eosinophilia, and acute toxemia—although you feel the chances are good that you will survive and live to a ripe old age.

Alternatively, you can bypass the dense thickets of medical terminology and go straight to the things that *everybody* understands: blood, sweat, pus, vomit, and diarrhea. When any two or more of these elements are present in an excuse, especially in an unusual and disgusting combination, you can rest assured that not only will the excuse be believed but it will also discourage any further inquiry into your condition.

This is not to say that you may have to be obscene to be believed. On the contrary, such is the general level of prudery in our society that all you need to make a medical excuse instantly acceptable is the mention of a urologist, a gynecologist, a proctologist—any specialist will do so long as he specializes in disorders of the naughty parts. Similarly, the vaguest reference to problems "down there," if delivered with the proper degree of implied embarrassment, will suffice to ensure the rapid acceptance of your excuse.

Finally, there is one medical excuse that shares with all the familial excuses the advantage of a built-in scapegoat—in this case, your doctor. It's surprising what you can get away with under the heading of "Doctor's Orders."

THE METEOROLOGICAL EXCUSE

The strength of the meteorological excuse is that it can be independently verified. That is also its weakness, because what *you* consider a torrential downpour might be seen by others as a light shower. Moreover, people such as your in-laws have a way of remembering how you used to drive through blizzards and ice storms when you were courting their daughter, and yet now a few snowflakes are enough to keep you indoors—especially if there is a good game on television.

Another drawback to the meteorological excuse is that, with a few exceptions, it has a short life span. Yesterday's rain won't help get you out of today's appointment, nor will tomorrow morning's anticipated snowfall release you from tomorrow afternoon's commitment. The rain or snow has to be coming down now, or to have just stopped, if it is to contribute to a convincing excuse.

There are, nonetheless, three ways in which the meteorological excuse can be used to good effect. One is by citing climatic extremes: earthquakes, floods, avalanches, mudslides. Natural disasters always make for excellent excuses so long as there are no hostile witnesses around to contradict your testimony.

The second way is to go to the opposite extreme: The weather was *too good.* If this sounds a little farfetched as the basis for an excuse, remember that the owners of the *Titanic* made precisely this claim to explain why their unsinkable ship unfortunately sank. Because the sea was *so* calm, they said with perfectly straight faces, there were *no* waves breaking around the base of the iceberg, and therefore the captain wasn't able to spot the iceberg in the darkness until it was too late.

Now, while it is hoped that you will not have any mishaps of this magnitude to explain away, you can still adapt the *form* of the excuse to your personal needs. For instance, you will almost certainly be forgiven for declining to indulge in even the gentlest activity when you explain that in your zeal to take advantage of the beautiful weather you managed to get your buttocks horribly sunburnt. You can even offer to provide proof of your condition, secure in the knowledge that the offer will be refused.

The third way to maximize the potential of the meteorological excuse is to use it in combination with another category, such as the familial:

> *My wife still isn't back yet. I expect she got caught in the rain and decided to wait until it ended.*

> *It was such a lovely day that the kids went swimming and my guess is that they just lost all track of the time.*

Or the financial:

> *With the roads so slippery, I'm nervous about driving until I can pay to have my brakes fixed.*

Or the medical:

> *It was so bright and sunny yesterday that I stupidly went out without a jacket, and today I'm in bed with a fever feeling lousy AND stupid.*

In the last resort, there is a medico-meteorological hybrid form which, if used judiciously, can prove most effective. It involves the invocation of certain medically recognized phobias that may arise in response to specific meteorological phenomena. These phobias, one might say, represent the last word in being "under the weather":

FEAR OF . . .	MEDICAL TERM
heat	thermophobia
cold	cheimaphobia
rain	ombrophobia
wind	anemophobia
fog	homichlophobia
thunder	brontophobia
lightning	astraphobia
floods	antlophobia
snow	chionphobia

You see, the weather doesn't have to be either good or bad to supply the foundation for an excuse. It just has to be scary.

THE TECHNOLOGICAL EXCUSE

The technological excuse, while it traffics in complexities beyond the understanding of most mortals, is actually the simplest to deliver. Something broke, that's all. And not only does this excuse have the beauty of simplicity, but it is accessible to anyone who occupies a dwelling more advanced than a cave, or who depends for transport on a vehicle more sophisticated than a tricycle, or who is daily exposed to any of those miracles of modern living— electricity, indoor plumbing, kitchen appliances, clocks, telephones—that are periodically subject to mechanical failure.

So numerous and so obvious are the possibilities for constructing a successful excuse on the ruins of a once-trusted object that it would be superfluous to list examples. In any case, it doesn't much matter what you blame, or for what. It only matters that the damn thing broke.

THE CALENDARIAL EXCUSE

The calendarial excuses are also numerous, but their number can be computed more exactly. There are precisely 365 of them (366 in a leap year), numbered 1 to 31. With these excuses you don't need to conjure up a sick child, or a burst pipe, or an overdrawn bank account. All you need is a date: The 14th is bad for you, the 23rd is out of the question, the 28th is booked solid, Thursdays are always difficult, and so forth. God knows, you *want* to clean the garage, or visit your mother, or clear up your debt, or take the kids to see a movie; it's just that the *timing* is a problem. It's a shame, really, because practically any other time . . .

The great thing about the calendarial excuse is that, like those notes you used to bring your teacher, *you have it in writing*. Never mind that the writing is in your own hand, and in your own diary, if indeed it exists at all. For some unknown reason, people who are disinclined to believe that you have the flu, even in season, are quite willing to accept that you have an upcoming audience with the Pope, provided you preface the announcement with the words, "Let me just check my diary."

The artful excuse-maker will help himself by purchasing only those appointment diaries which take note of every conceivable holiday and holy day
in the known world. To these commemorative occasions you can then add
every birthday and anniversary that you can remember, plus such recurring
inconveniences as can be predicted on the basis of your biorhythm chart,
your menstrual cycle, or your horoscope.

Having done that, if your calendar or diary still has what Alexander Haig
used to call "windows of vulnerability," you have at your disposal a number
of seasonal excuses. Like the "moveable feasts" on liturgical calendars,
these can be moved around from year to year, depending on the date for
which you are most in need of an excuse. For example, at any time during
the first quarter of the year it is not unreasonable to suppose that you may
be busy preparing your taxes. During the second quarter, spring cleaning (or
gardening, if you're the outdoor type) might easily obliterate an entire week.
Then comes the third quarter, encompassing both conventional vacation
time and back-to-school time, both of which can eat into anyone's schedule,
while the fourth quarter is of course darkened by the looming specter of
Christmas. With the right calendar you can have a busy year.

And even without a calendar you can always be *potentially* busy whenever an unappealing prospect comes along. All you have to do is recite the
magic words, "I don't have my diary with me at the moment—let me get
back to you on this." And of course when you get back to them an engagement has appeared on your calendar which, shucks, spoils everything. (It
can even spoil things in retrospect: "Are you *sure* you said Wednesday the
17th? Funny, I have it written down for Wednesday the 24th. Oh well, it's
been that kind of month.") One word of caution, however. Because of the
vast potential of the yet-to-be-consulted diary, you should never carry one on
your person. Even a half-blind illiterate knows a blank page when he sees
one.

* * * * *

In addition to these six types of excuses, there are a number of all-purpose
excuses that you should keep warm and ready at all times should you ever
find yourself stuck without a good categorical one. Unlike the excuses we

have considered so far, the all-purpose excuses do not vary according to the circumstances or people involved, nor are they open to corroboration or dispute. Indeed, they are specifically designed to close off further discussion of any kind. They are nonnegotiable. And final.

When used to get out of doing something, they are introduced by one of the following phrases:

> *I'm sorry, but I never . . .*
>
> *Thank you, but I don't . . .*
>
> *I refuse on principle to . . .*
>
> *I make it a rule not to . . .*
>
> *I promised my wife/husband that, whatever happens, I wouldn't . . .*
>
> *You must be kidding, I didn't think ANYONE . . .*

When it comes to getting out of trouble for something you've already done, the best (if not the only) all-purpose excuse is a vow of silence. Angry, wounded silence:

> *If you really believe that I would be capable of _____, then there's no point in even talking about it.*
>
> *I can explain everything, but I'm not going to until you're at least prepared to listen.*
>
> *I refuse to discuss it when you're in this mood.*

If you have the psychological stamina to follow up your vow of silence with a prolonged sulk, so much the better. You might even succeed ultimately in having yourself reclassified as the injured party. But at the very least this kind of off-the-rack excuse will buy you the time to come up with one precisely tailored to fit the individual situation.

The use of the sartorial metaphor here is deliberate, because however good the material from which you fashion your excuse, unless it matches the circumstances to which you apply it, you may well end up by making the situation even more difficult than it already is. As Pembroke shrewdly observed to Salisbury in Shakespeare's *King John*:

> . . . oftentimes excusing of a fault
> Doth make the fault the worse by the excuse,
> As patches set upon a little breach
> Discredit more in hiding of the fault
> Than did the fault before it was so patch'd.

Thus to become a skillful patcher of breaches one must have a proper regard not only for what goes into the making of an excuse—whether it be faulty plumbing or faulty children—but also for *how* the excuse is made. To this end I have devised a set of rules, which I modestly call the Ten Commandments, to guide those who would follow in the path of the truly great excuse-makers—which is of course the path marked "Exit."

Abide by these and, I assure you, your life will be at once more entertaining and less complicated.

I   *Thou shalt not hold thy tongue until it is too late*

With the making of excuses, timing is crucial. In this respect the recipe for a good excuse is exactly like the recipe for a good soufflé: Whatever the ingredients, *serve immediately*. The longer the excuse has to cool, the greater the chance that it will collapse. And then you have to find an excuse for *that.*

This applies equally to the preemptive and the exculpatory excuses. In the case of the former (which can become the latter if you wait too long), it's easier to explain why you *can't* than it is to explain why you *didn't*. With the latter, it's a lot easier to explain why you did something than it is to explain why you didn't bother explain sooner why you did something. This is known as the Chappaquiddick Principle. To this day a cloud of suspicion shadows Senator Kennedy not because he gave an implausible version of the events that night on the island, but because he waited until the next morning to give it.

So unless there are special circumstances that dictate otherwise, it is important to register your excuse as early as possible. In fact, when con-

fronted by people who you have reason to believe are going to propose something unappealing, or who might be tempted to accuse you of something
unappealing, it is not a bad idea to register your excuse in advance. Thus
when they greet you with the perfunctory "How are you?", seize the opportunity to tell them just how wretched things are for you at the moment. Or
you may simply hint that things are not going well, as W.C. Fields did whenever someone said "Good morning." His classic reply: "Don't jump to con-
clusions."

Either way—inventorying your problems or merely hinting at their existence—you are laying an unshakable foundation for an excuse, because it
will be in place *before* the excuse is needed.

II   *Thou shalt employ thy tongue in a convincing manner*

As important as your timing is your tone of voice when delivering an
excuse. With one exception—when abject confusion is itself part of the excuse—you must avoid sounding tentative or uncertain. If by your manner
you make it appear that you are offering the excuse on a trial basis, you will
immediately be suspected of dissembling.

The situation of the would-be excuse-maker is exactly that of an actor. If
either delivers his lines badly, haltingly, he will fail to engage the sympathy
of his audience; he may even destroy what Coleridge called the audience's
"willing suspension of disbelief." Therefore the good maker of excuses, like
the good actor, will always see to it that the presentation of the excuse is
appropriate to its contents.

Because the best excuses are those that induce a strong emotional response—preferably of identification ("I know how you feel") or of guilt ("I
certainly didn't mean to *add* to your worries . . .")—they should be delivered
in a manner designed to stimulate the desired response.

In some cases, for example, you will want to convey an impression of
disappointment and frustration, even anger. This means that if you choose a
medical excuse, say, to avoid eating a particular food, you ought to put some
feeling into it. Instead of saying weakly, "I'm not supposed to eat that," you
curse your luck: "Wouldn't you know it! My *favorite!* God, I could strangle
my doctor for prescribing those damned pills." Similarly, should you opt for

a technological excuse to explain why you missed an important appointment, you don't want to refer limply to "car trouble," you want to rage maniacally against the nest of thieves and saboteurs whom you just paid a fortune to repair the godforsaken machine.

Alternatively, you might want to give the impression that your suffering is already so great that only a sadist would risk making it worse by, for instance, insisting on repayment of an ancient loan, or demanding to know how you happened to park the car in the swimming pool. For this you will need to whip yourself into a frenzy of self-accusation and self-flagellation so brutal that your erstwhile tormentor is moved to utter the sacred incantation, "Come on now, you're being too hard on yourself." Which of course you are. That's the whole point. Just don't let them catch you grinning in triumph afterward.

III *Thou shalt honor thy Ma Bell*

In evolutionary terms, the invention of the telephone may well turn out to be *the* pivotal event in the fulfillment of our biological destiny as a species. Consider, for a moment, what makes us unique among the higher primates. It's not our ability to make tools, as some people still seem to believe; there are other species with the ability to make tools. *It's our ability to make excuses!* That's what sets us apart. Any monkey can make a tool of some kind, but no monkey ever came swinging home at five in the morning with a story about being detained by a bunch of mean-looking tigers hanging out at the corner of a nearby clearing.

Still, it was only with the invention of the telephone barely a century ago that we began to realize our full potential as makers of excuses. For the telephone is, without question, the ideal instrument for delivering an excuse. To begin with, it eliminates the need to account for contradictory visual evidence, such as someone in the bed next to you at the time that you're having a "critical business meeting," or the golf clubs leaning against the door as you enter the terminal stages of mononucleosis.

Furthermore, telephone testimony is not subject to cross-examination because it can be terminated at will: All of a sudden you hear the doorbell ring, or you smell something burning, or your other telephone rings (nice touch). And, in extreme circumstances, you can always be "cut off"—so long as you are careful to pull the plug on yourself in mid-sentence.

In addition, for special occasions there is a unique device, one that was clearly created with no other purpose in mind than to elevate our credibility as an excuse-making species. It is called the pay telephone, and it is available on street corners throughout the world. This miraculous contraption makes it possible for you to deliver your excuse with whatever background sound effects you may need—from wailing sirens to shouting voices—in order to give your story the right flavor and urgency.

Nor is the telephone's usefulness limited to the transmission of excuses. It can be an excuse in itself. All you need is to arrange for someone to call you shortly after you've arrived for something you want to get out of—a party, a dinner, a meeting, a visit, an assignation, whatever. Upon being given the telephone, you simply pause for a few moments, just long enough to let your features darken with distress, then you utter a suitable phrase (something along the lines of "Oh my God, I'll be there as soon as I can"), and—presto!—you're free.

Finally, even a telephone that hasn't rung can provide an excuse: "I'm afraid I have to stay here by the telephone. I'm expecting an important long-distance call." Wonderful instrument, the telephone.

IV   *Thou shalt not hesitate to point thy finger*

Whatever the circumstances you invoke in the making of an excuse, you should never lose sight of the fact that one of the main purposes of an excuse is to place the blame on someone else. Or on something, anything, so long as it is outside your control. The only time you take full responsibility for not doing something, or for having done something, is when you can imply that the blame really belongs elsewhere, but that you are taking it yourself out of sheer magnanimity of spirit: "It's entirely my own fault. I knew I was taking a risk, but sometimes you just to have to trust people . . ." Or words to that effect.

Even the most convincing excuse—an attack of pneumonia, an attack of in-laws—is improved by subtle finger-pointing: It's not you but your child who has pneumonia (probably after ignoring pleas to dress warmly), it's your wife who invited her parents for a visit (against your wishes), and so on.

But to be effective, the finger you point must not be too obvious. A crudely pointed finger is like a carelessly thrown boomerang. It can have harsher consequences for you than for its intended target. This is why history's earliest recorded excuse was such a dismal failure. When God asked Adam why he had disobeyed and eaten the forbidden fruit, he immediately pointed at Eve and said, "The woman . . . *she* gave me of the tree." Whereupon Eve pointed at the snake and blamed *him*: "The serpent beguiled me," she claimed innocently. Needless to say, Adam and Eve both got evicted from Eden, and rightly so, because they insulted their humanity by making dreadful excuses.

Nonetheless, the precedent they set was a good one, and it is still observed today by the most skilled practitioners of the art of excuse-making. To take a recent example, when New York senatorial candidate Bruce Caputo was caught lying about his wartime service in the army, he defended himself thus: "To the extent that I *or somebody on my staff* was less than careful, *we* made a mistake." (The italics you see are mine, but the finger you see behind them is Mr. Caputo's.)

Of course, the undisputed world champion at wrapping an excuse around a pointed finger is Richard Nixon. Now retired, he successfully defended his title many times, but never more brilliantly than when he explained Watergate in a televised interview with David Frost:

> I'm convinced that if it hadn't been for Martha [Mitchell], and God rest her soul, because she, in her heart, was a good person. She just had a mental and emotional problem that nobody knew about. If it hadn't been for Martha, there'd have been no Watergate, because John wasn't minding that store. He was letting Magruder and all these kids, these nuts, run this thing. Now, am I saying here, at this juncture, that Watergate should be blamed on Martha Mitchell? Of course not. I'm trying to explain my feeling of compassion for my friend, John Mitchell.

Now *there* is a great master at work.

During his long and distinguished career as a finger-pointer, Mr. Nixon's only weakness, if one can speak thus of someone so unnaturally gifted, was his flawed sense of timing. He always had a tendency to wait just a bit too long before suddenly wheeling with flared nostrils and thrusting a quivering digit in the direction of his daughter's cocker spaniel or his attorney general's dead wife. It could be argued, I suppose, that as a consummate excuse-maker he was simply saving his best for last. Still, one can't help but feel that he would have been even more effective had he landed his punch lines earlier.

Indeed, he might have taken a leaf out of Henry Kissinger's book, *Years of Upheaval*, in which the wily former Nixon associate expounds eloquently on the importance of keeping a finger cocked in advance, ready for pointing at the first sign of trouble. Discussing a letter that Nixon sent to Brezhnev in October 1973, prior to Dr. Kissinger's arrival in the Soviet Union for talks on the Yom Kippur War, Dr. Kissinger writes: "Its essence was that Nixon was granting me 'full authority.' I was horrified. I would be deprived of any capacity to stall. . . . History will not record that I resisted many grants of authority. This one I resented bitterly. . . ."

No wonder. The "good guy–bad guy" routine is a mainstay of every excuse-maker's repertoire, so if you are without even the threat of a bad guy lurking in the wings, someone with whom you have to clear any commitments you make, your room to maneuver, like Dr. Kissinger's in the Kremlin, will be severely restricted. You should always maintain a supporting cast of people whom at any given time you may have to "check with first."

It is also worth noting that as long as the finger of blame points away from you, it doesn't automatically have to point *at* someone else. It can be waved vaguely at impersonal forces hiding somewhere inside the grammar of your excuse. A classic example of this kind of vague finger-pointing and shoulder-shrugging was the Japanese government's bulletin announcing its surrender in 1945. It avoided saying anything as straightforward as "They won" or as self-incriminating as "We lost." Instead it said: "The war situation has developed not necessarily to Japan's advantage." That is so beautiful it could be a Zen haiku.

On a less exalted plane, but with the same tactical intent, my six-year-old son came to me one day with the information, "There's milk on the kitchen floor."

"Oh there is, is there?" I said, trying not to look amused or overly admiring of his technique. "And why is that?"

"It accidentally spilled," he deadpanned.

"I see. *It* spilled." By now I was curious to see how long he could keep it up. "I don't suppose by any chance you were with the milk when it had its accident?"

"Of course," he said in a tone of weary exasperation. "That's how I know it spilled. I just thought I should tell you. . . ." His voice trailed off, as did he, leaving behind the clear implication that if I wasn't interested in household accidents he wouldn't bother in future to keep me informed. I cleaned up the milk.

V   *Thou shalt endeavor to be topical*

In an age dominated by the electronic news media, people are increasingly reluctant to believe even the evidence of their own senses unless and until it is corroborated by radio or television. Therefore it is helpful, though by no means obligatory, to link your excuse in some way to an event or situation that is in the news. Strikes, epidemics, power failures, explosions, earthquakes, crime waves, really big fires, assassination attempts, bomb threats—these are all grist for the milling of excuses.

The supreme virtue of topicality is that it distracts attention away from the essentials of the excuse and shifts it to the extraneous circumstances, thereby adding a dash of glamour to even the most humdrum excuses. For example, the same people who are unmoved by your tale of a terrible traffic jam will suddenly become fascinated upon hearing that the traffic jam was caused by a motorcade for a visiting potentate, or by a political demonstration, or by a spectacularly gruesome crash, or by you-don't-know-what but you know there certainly were a lot of TV cameras around and you can't wait to watch the news tonight.

Likewise, the person who fails to register any sympathetic concern over the fact that your daughter is late in returning the car will almost certainly become concerned when you add that she had to go into an area where your local Hillside Strangler or Yorkshire Ripper has been active recently. And while having to wait for a long-distance call may not be a compelling excuse in itself, it begins to become one when you explain that the call you are waiting for is from a friend who is free-lancing as a photographer in Lebanon (or El Salvador, or Angola, or Afghanistan, or Poland, or the trouble spot of your choice).

VI *Thou shalt not withhold any details*

A few years ago when I was putting together my collection of funny hate mail, *Dear Sir, Drop Dead!*, I debated at some length whether to include letters written to institutions. It seemed to me that these letters, written mostly to businesses and alleging everything from incompetent service to outright fraud, lacked the colorful vituperation of the letters written to individuals, and at the same time were overloaded with endless details of the frustrations and indignities suffered by the correspondents. In the end, however, I decided that they belonged in the book.

It was a happy decision, for these letters turned out to be among the most popular in the collection. And the reason they were so widely enjoyed, it finally dawned on me, was that precisely *because* they were so detailed they struck a responsive chord in most readers. Regardless of the subject matter, each letter had *something* in it, some harrowing little detail, that the ordinary person could readily identify with.

The lesson here is obvious: When offering an excuse, don't be stingy with the details. Not only do they lend credibility to your story, but they give it a narrative force that involves the listener and takes his mind off the fact that it *is* an excuse. Say, for example, you find yourself in a situation that calls for a financial excuse. While it may be sufficient merely to cite your insolvency, the excuse will be much improved if you spice it up with details of some of the embarrassing economies you've been forced to make, the evasive tactics you've employed to dodge creditors, the late-night raids you've made on your kid's piggy bank, the things you've learned from reading about bankruptcy procedures, and so on.

To see just how engrossing an excuse can be when no detail is spared, consider the following excerpt from a letter written some years ago by a bricklayer in London to explain to his employer why he had failed to show up for work. His basic excuse was medical—he had been hospitalized due to injuries he had received while on the job—but he didn't just leave it at that. He went on to explain the circumstances of his accident:

*When I got to the top of the building, I found that the
hurricane had knocked some bricks off the top. So I rigged up
a beam, with a pulley, at the top of the building, and hoisted
up a couple of barrels full of bricks. When I had fixed the
building, there was a lot of bricks left over, so I hoisted the
barrel back up again, and secured the line at the bottom, and
then went up and filled the barrel with the extra bricks. Then I
went to the bottom and cast off the line. Unfortunately the
barrel of bricks was heavier than I was and before I knew what
was happening the barrel started down, jerking me off the
ground. I decided to hang on, and halfway up I met the barrel
coming down and received a severe blow on the shoulder. I
then continued to the top, banging my head against the beam
and getting my fingers jammed in the pulley. When the barrel
hit the ground it burst at its bottom, allowing all the bricks to
spill out. I was now heavier than the barrel and so started
down again at high speed. Halfway down I met the barrel
coming up and received severe injury to my shins. When I hit
the ground I landed on the bricks, getting several painful cuts
from the sharp edges. At this point I must have lost my
presence of mind because I let go the line. The barrel then
came down, giving me another heavy blow on the head and
putting me in hospital.*

That, by anyone's standards, is a four-star excuse.

VII   *Thou shalt not kill with solemnity*

As the bricklayer's letter so splendidly illustrates, an excuse that moves
you to laughter can be just as effective as one that moves you to tears—
indeed more so, because with humor you can win the listener's sympathy
and gratitude. This is the Banana Peel Principle. While we sympathize with
someone who had the bad luck to slip on a banana peel, either literally or
figuratively, we are nonetheless grateful for the chance to laugh at someone
else's misfortune.

So, whenever possible, do some entertaining with your explaining.

VIII   *Thou shalt observe the Law of Inverse Credibility*

For reasons not immediately apparent, there is a widespread tendency among otherwise rational people to disbelieve the most credible excuses and to believe unhesitatingly the most incredible ones. Thus "My bus was late" is greeted with a derisive smirk, while "The bus was attacked by Palestinians and I was the sole survivor" is received with a horrified gasp of solicitude. And people whose eyelids would droop at the news that your cat was hit by a car will suddenly have dilated pupils on hearing that your cat was hit by sniper fire.

Here you see the Law of Inverse Credibility at work. According to this law, the more improbable your excuse the greater the probability that people will believe it—on the grounds that you couldn't have made up something so improbable. Children understand this, in a rudimentary way; that's why they are always claiming that "the dog ate my homework." Christopher Ward, a columnist for the London *Daily Mirror,* understands it in a more sophisticated way; that's why he always screams "Bloody dogs!" whenever he bounces his car off oncoming traffic. Mr. Ward reckons that on a good day he can persuade up to three eyewitnesses that they actually saw a phantom hound speed in front of his vehicle, causing him to swerve. "And one of them," he says, "will even know whose dog it was."

When it comes to the making of baroque excuses, however, even the invisible dog makes a rather primitive scapegoat compared to other creatures. Remember when President Carter claimed to have been attacked by a killer rabbit? That was probably the finest hour of his presidency. Pause for a moment and reflect: If you claim to have been stalked by a killer, people will simply think you are paranoid. If you claim that you were stalked by a rabbit, they will assume you are on drugs. But to have been stalked and molested by a killer rabbit—who wouldn't be eager to hear the details of *that* experience? It's a shame that Mr. Carter didn't get a second term so that we could see what else he could pull out of his hat.

An outstanding example of the Killer Rabbit excuse occurred recently at the murder trial of a Virginia man who had killed his mother-in-law in the garage with a hatchet. His excuse was that he mistook her for a raccoon. Now he could easily have said that he mistook her for an intruder, or perhaps an unidentifiable monster. But no. A raccoon. History, alas, does not record what the jurors made of this, but they should have stood and applauded.

In any case, the point is that when the stakes are high it is generally better to reject the little white lie in favor of the big purple one, especially if you introduce it by: "You won't believe this, but . . ."

They'll believe it every time.

IX   *Thou shalt observe the Law of Diminishing Returns*

There is an old joke about a defendant who failed to turn up in court one day.

When asked by the judge to explain his client's absence, the defense lawyer replied, "There are three reasons, Your Honor. First, he died last night. Second, . . ." At which point the judge interrupted: "You may dispense with the other two."

Like the lawyer, you should resist the temptation to offer supplementary excuses. One is enough, if it's good. And if it's not good, you won't improve it by piling on added excuses. If you feel that your allergy is an inadequate excuse for not doing something, then come up with a better one. Don't add that you are also broke, and your car is in the shop, and the maid just quit, and the chimney is on fire.

Any time you resort to multiple excuses, each one casts doubt on the veracity of the one that preceded it. And it only takes one excuse too many to demolish your credibility.

X   *Thou shalt sow even as thou reap*

Lastly, when making excuses you should be mindful of the generations of excuses yet unborn. The right excuse can bear fruit repeatedly in future situations; the wrong excuse can come back to haunt you. For instance, if someone has been pestering you to join in an activity that you know takes place only at lunchtime, or only on Monday, then you want an excuse that covers *all* lunchtimes or *all* Mondays (if it doesn't cover the activity itself). If you use an excuse that covers only one specific date, you will have to think of another excuse, and another, and another, if the invitation is repeated. Thus you will end up ensnared in the multiple-excuse trap.

Or suppose that someone you wish to avoid is pressuring you for a meeting next week. Of course the best excuse is that you will be away next week—out of town, out of the country, wherever—but even this can be improved by a little forward planning. You might say, for example, that the trip couldn't have come at a worse time for you, as you are already far behind in your work—thereby setting up a "work-load" excuse for your return, just in case there is still time left for the unwanted meeting. And you might add that, to compound your frustration, you don't even know how long you will have to be away—thereby reserving to yourself the responsibility for making contact on your return.

Although any type of excuse can be used to plant the seeds of later excuses, the medical category is particularly fertile because it includes so many chronic conditions. However, it must be remembered that for a chronic condition to be useful as a chronic excuse, the *symptoms* must be chronic as well. It's no good getting migraines only when your mate makes amorous approaches, or getting muscle spasms only when asked to clean out the basement or mow the lawn. These little coincidences do not go unnoticed, or unpunished. Therefore you would be wise to keep your medical excuses healthy, as it were, by wincing in agony from time to time as a reminder to others of the serious nature of the condition on which you base your excuses.

But whatever the category from which you choose your excuse in a given situation, the important thing to keep in mind is that if you want the excuse to enjoy a long and productive life, without trespassing on the claims of other valuable excuses, you have to plan ahead.

A good excuse in time saves nine. Or more.

PART ONE

GETTING OUT OF...

. . . Social Engagements

Social engagements all have one thing in common: a set time and place. Not surprisingly, then, the most fruitful category from which to choose an excuse for getting out of such engagements is the calendarial:

> *Wouldn't you know it? That's the one night this week we're busy.*

> *Alas, I have to go and play backgammon with my boss on the 10th. And as much as I hate backgammon, I do like my job.*

> *We always go and visit my parents on Sundays.*

> *I just bought tickets for the opera that evening. If only you'd called earlier. . . .*

But what if you think you might want to attend a function after you find out more about it? In that case you give the same kind of excuse, but provisionally:

> *I'm supposed to take the kids to the planetarium on Saturday, but maybe there's some way I can get out of it.*

> *I know Mary wants to go and see the new Truffaut film that evening, but I think I might be able to talk her out of it.*

> *I'm afraid the 4th is going to be difficult, unless I can switch something around. Anyway, let me see what I can do.*

Having thus signaled your eagerness to be a part of the occasion to which you have been invited, you can proceed to make subtle inquiries as to the precise nature of the occasion: what is going to be served (or discussed, or shown, or performed, or whatever), how long it will last, who else is going to be there, and so forth. With this information you will then be able to decide whether or not you want to attend. If you do, you will earn bonus points when you call back to accept because of all the trouble you have gone to in order to be there. And if you don't, you will still get credit for having tried.

With invitations and summonses issued at point-blank range—that is, within twenty-four hours of the occasion to be avoided—the other categories of excuses can be called upon. The familial, for instance:

> *I doubt that we can get a babysitter at such short notice.*

> *My sister is on her way over here. Her rat of a husband just left her and I have to try to cheer her up.*

The financial:

> *I'm afraid we're keeping a low profile at the moment, due to what the bank calls "insufficient funds."*

> *If I come, can you lend me some money?*

The medical:

> *Right now, I'd throw up at the very sight of food. I had clams for dinner last night, and they must have been off because I've been in the bathroom ever since I woke up. Don't ask why.*

> *Want to hear something ridiculous? I was blinded by the cat this morning. That's right. While I was washing my face the stupid beast jumped up on the counter beside the sink where I had put my glasses. The glasses ended up on the floor, in little pieces. I kept the pieces so that I can grind them up and sprinkle them in the cat's food. Anyway, I can't see a thing. . . .*

The meteorological:

Are you crazy? Have you been outside?

I'll do it if you'll send someone over to empty the pots and pans that I've spread around to catch the drips.

The technological:

That's when the man is supposed to come and fix the air conditioning. He said he would be here sometime between one and six, which probably means 5:55, but I can't take a chance on missing him or I'll have to sweat out another week.

Remember that bout of diarrhea I had last week that kept me from going to the game with you? No, I'm feeling all right now, but the toilet chose today as the day to get revenge. There's water everywhere.

In addition to these categorical excuses, there are the all-purpose excuses, any one of which can be adapted to suit the occasion-to-be-missed. For example:

Thank you, but I don't dance.

I make it a rule to keep the weekends free for my family.

I refuse on principle to go to cocktail parties.

You know me well enough to know that I never go out when I have a project to finish.

Or you may wish to try an amusing variant of the all-purpose excuse, in which case you could do worse than follow the example of Lord Charles Beresford (1846–1919) when he was summoned to dine with the Prince of Wales. His reply, by telegram: "VERY SORRY CAN'T COME. LIE FOLLOWS BY POST." Funnier still was the excuse given recently by an Anglo-Indian author in London upon being invited to a dinner party the following week. He declined on the grounds that he wasn't hungry.

The fact that these two excuses were accepted without question or resentment—on the contrary, the spurned hosts delighted in quoting them for the entertainment of others—shows that if your excuse is amusing enough, people will ignore the purpose it serves and treasure it for its own sake.

While most social invitations come with some form of enticement—a free dinner, free drinks, theatre tickets, a day in the country, a ride to the beach—there are people, usually the most resistible, who rely not on enticement but on entrapment to draw you into their orbit. Instead of asking, "Would you like to go to a movie?", they ask, "What are you doing right now?" They never say, "Let's get together for a game of cards Thursday night"; rather, they inquire, "Are you doing anything Thursday night?" In other words, they try to pry loose an admission of your availability *before* proposing a social activity.

The best way of dealing with these despicable lowlifes is by showing your contempt for their ploy:

> *Are you taking a poll, or did you have something in mind?*

> *I think I probably am, but you can try anyway.*

> *That depends. Make me an offer.*

Then, when the offer turns out to be one you can refuse, as it inevitably will be, you can pull out any of a number of conventional excuses. It doesn't even have to be clever or original. After all, they know it's coming; otherwise they wouldn't have tried to sneak around it in the first place.

Finally, what if you have accepted an invitation to an event *faute de mieux*, on the off-chance that it might prove interesting, and then want to get out of it once you're there? The handiest escape route is via the telephone. At a prearranged time it rings with some bad news which sends you scurrying homeward, aflame with worry. Or you can dial the bad news yourself—"I just want to give the babysitter a call to make sure everything's okay, it's the first time she's been with the kids, you know"—and when there is no answer at the number you dialed you make a hasty yet dignified exit. At best, you will leave everyone impressed with your self-control under stress. At least, you will leave everyone.

Such, indeed, is the versatility of the telephone that it can come in handy even when you're *not* yet ready to make your escape. Simply by saying into the receiver, "Call me back in an hour unless there's been a sudden change for the worse," or by muttering aloud, as if trying to convince yourself, "The babysitter probably couldn't hear the phone because the bathwater was running," you will not only generate waves of sympathy for your predicament, but when you do depart, perhaps after the next phone call, you will leave behind a group burning with vicarious anxiety and at the same time glowing with the compliment you have paid them by staying so long. This is what's known in some circles as a no-lose situation.

However, if you don't like working with props, you can always invoke the name of The One You Left Behind—babysitter, mate, house guest—as an excuse for leaving early:

> *What time do you have? Christ, I promised I would be home*
> *by now. Maybe I should phone and say I'm on my way. No,*
> *I'll just make a dash for it.*

And then there's the excuse provided by sudden internal sabotage:

> *Do you have some place where I could lie down for a few*
> *minutes? I'm all right, really, just a bit dizzy. I'm sure I'll feel*
> *better in a little while.*

A little while later, of course, you are not feeling much better—just strong enough to leave. Whereupon you mumble your dazed apologies and walk slowly,

       feebly,

          out.

EXCUSES YOU SHOULD NEVER USE FOR GETTING OUT OF SOCIAL ENGAGEMENTS
. . . and the reasons why

I won't know anybody there.
You're scared of meeting new people? Where you do you go on vacation—next door?

We're having a dinner party ourselves that evening.
And, they will note, you didn't think to invite them.

I've already seen that movie.
Which only leaves 283 other movies for them to choose from.

That's the night we always stay home and watch TV.
If you're really trying to be insulting, you might as well say that you want to stay home in case the phone rings.

We've been out late so much recently that by tommorow we will be ready for an early night.
Translation: We will accept any invitation except yours.

... Domestic Chores

Getting out of household chores is a difficult business for even the most proficient excuse-makers. For one thing, the competition is stiff: Everyone else in the house wants out of the chores, too. For another thing, unlike most other activities and situations, domestic chores don't go away; they wait patiently for you. Finally, because any excuse you offer is perforce intramural, and thus subject to immediate verification, your scope for inventiveness is severely limited.

Indeed, the criteria for a convincing excuse are so stringent that four entire categories of excuses are rendered virtually useless. The familial, for example, isn't going to be much help when the person to whom you give the excuse is almost certain to be a member of your family. Granted, you may be able to get out of washing the car by saying you promised to take the kids to the park, but the car will still be dirty when you get back.

Likewise, the meteorological, technological, and calendarial categories are all ineffective due to the stubborn refusal of domestic chores to disappear. You may get out of mowing the lawn on the grounds that the grass is too wet, or the sun too hot, but the grass will dry out and the sun will set. Then what? Or you may get out of cleaning the carpet by claiming that the vacuum cleaner isn't working properly, but it can easily be fixed. And you may be excused from certain chores because it's a special or unusual day, but there's always tomorrow and tomorrow and tomorrow.

In other words, with the excuses in these categories the best you can do is win a postponement. And even that can hardly be counted a victory, because the longer you postpone a domestic chore the more unpleasant it gets. The dishes multiply, the weeds spread, the floor gets dirtier, the grass gets longer, the dust gets thicker, the snow gets higher, the garbage gets smellier.

This leaves only two categories that can supply you with a satisfactory excuse when confronted with the dread specter of housework or yard work: the financial and the medical. And even within these two your choices are restricted.

The financial excuse depends for its effectiveness on the subtle suggestion that it would be a criminal misallocation of the family's resources for you to waste your time in menial labor when you should be concentrating on matters pertaining to the security and well-being of your loved ones. This is achieved by ducking behind a mountain range of paper—bills, receipts, checkbooks, statements, tax records, investment portfolios, life insurance brochures, retirement account prospectuses, anything with numbers on it— where you can take shelter whenever a domestic chore raises its ugly head:

> *I was trying to find a way to provide for the kids' college education, but if it's more important to you that I trim the hedges, okay, fine. When they graduate from high school we'll give each one a framed picture of the hedges.*

> *You keep asking me if we will have enough money to live on when we retire, yet whenever I start to work on the answer you want me to work on the attic.*

> *Look, if I'm not allowed to get our taxes done it won't MATTER whether the house is clean. We'll all be in jail.*

> *I know you don't like me to bring home work from the office. I don't like it either. But I have this silly notion that right now we will be better off if I keep my job than if I keep the weeds out of the flowerbed.*

> *All right, which would you rather have me do? Bring in the clothes off the line or try to bring in some money? It's up to you.*

The idea, obviously (though it shouldn't be made too obvious), is to foster the belief that you cannot reasonably be expected to focus your attention on the Higher Things, such as your family's economic future, if you are going to be harassed to perform lowly functions, such as taking out the garbage.

By contrast, the medical excuses are all reducible to a single syllable: *Aarrrgh!* It hurts too much. You want to help, but *it hurts too much.* What hurts? That's up to you, of course, but a cursory study of human anatomy would seem to suggest that a problem with the lower back is the most generally incapacitating. After that, the major joints are your best bet: hips, knees, ankles, elbows, wrists. But, once again, you mustn't forget to issue periodic reminders of your suffering. It's even worth offering to make the bed once in a while just so you have the opportunity to fall over in a pitiable heap, your face contorted in pain.

In those areas where you can't claim exemption on the basis of your physical disability—dishwashing and diaper-changing, to name only two— you can employ an all-purpose excuse so long as you establish early on that you *never* do dishes or that you *will not* change diapers. (Bill Cosby says that when his first child was born he informed his wife that under no circumstances would he change diapers. His reason: "I don't like surprises.") And once you have established what you won't do, you must never relent, even if it means that a penicillin culture forms around the ziggurat of dishes in the sink.

Still, the best way of getting out of domestic chores is to avoid being asked to do them in the first place. To this end, there are three strategies that you will find particularly rewarding. The first is the systematic cultivation of incompetence. Whatever you do around the house, do it badly. If you take out the garbage, leave a trail of coffee grounds and egg shells to commemorate your expedition. If you do the dishes, break a few while you're at it. If you clean the attic, accidentally throw out one of your mate's most cherished possessions. If you mow the lawn, cut down a few plants along with the grass. If you weed the flowerbed, pull out some of the flowers and leave some of the weeds. If you change the baby's diaper, spill its contents on the floor; if that doesn't work, next time spill the baby on the floor. Do whatever is necessary to make people think twice before asking you to perform a chore again.

The second strategy is to create the illusion of an equal division of labor. This is not as difficult as it may at first appear. The trick is to volunteer for little chores whenever it's easy for you to do them. For example, if you are getting up to go to the bathroom anyway, offer to check and see what the kids are doing. If your last meal consisted of sandwiches or a TV dinner, offer to do the dishes. If you are going to the garage to sneak a drink, offer to take out the garbage (especially if it's only half full). If you have to go out to place a quiet bet, offer to pick up something from the store. With each offer you get credit not only for sharing the work load, but also for your willingness to do your part.

Thirdly, you should develop the ability to anticipate the more excruciating chores so that you have time to take evasive action. This is not to say that you should simply vanish every time you see the fireplace filling up with ashes, or the sink filling up with dishes. In fact, it's wiser in the long run not to vanish when you see a nasty job looming but to occupy yourself with something considerably less taxing, such as cleaning the ashtrays or dusting the coffee table. That way you are already busy helping out when the really dirty work has to be done. And if you see the work coming well enough in advance, you can take the added precaution of showering and dressing in nice clean clothes—too nice and too clean to do any work in.

To sum up, then: Make sure that those who would press you into service around the house are continually aware that your mind is preoccupied with money worries, while your body is racked with pain. Whenever possible, volunteer for light duty to avoid being conscripted for heavy duty. Be alert to the danger of a potentially onerous task taking shape somewhere on the premises, so that you can be otherwise engaged when it threatens to ruin your day. And when, at last, you are faced with a chore that is impossible to escape, make such a botch of it that no one is ever tempted to ask you to do it again.

EXCUSES YOU SHOULD NEVER USE FOR GETTING OUT OF DOMESTIC CHORES
. . . and the reasons why

It's not my turn.
Very unwise, this, because it involves a tacit admission that you *have* a turn. This can cause you trouble later.

Why do I have to do most of the work around here?
You don't, if you have been at all successful with your excuses, and therefore it is not in your interest to encourage comparisons with others.

I just don't feel up to it today.
Who does? And what are you going to do about tomorrow?

Why can't YOU do it?
They will be more than happy to tell you.

That's not my job.
This inevitably leads to a discussion of which jobs *are* yours— a discussion to be avoided at all costs, unless you are better at negotiating than you are at making excuses.

. . . Awkward or Boring
Conversations

Like a plague of locusts, they swarm out of nowhere and land everywhere, infesting every corner of our existence, spreading with their mouths a fearful pestilence. They can go for hours without stopping for breath. Although their bite is not lethal, there is no known antidote for their bark. They can kill a healthy conversation in minutes.

They are the people who want to tell you their problems, people who will tell you what's the matter with you, people who want to talk about the weather, people who want to know how you made out last night, people who told you so, people who hope you've learned your lesson, people who want to know where you've been all their life, people who have been living in California, people who ask if you've heard the one about . . ., people who want to know how much you pull down in an average year, people who want to know where the broads are, people who want to know what you think of Ronald Reagan, people who want to know what your friend is like in bed, people who want to know what a nice girl like you is doing in a place like this, people who "don't mean to be personal, but . . .", people who want to know what it's like being Jewish, or tall, or gay, or famous, or convicted.

You know the people I'm talking about. Unfortunately, however, you don't often recognize them until they open their mouths—and then it's too late to reroute yourself out of range of their voices. So if you are to survive an encounter with them—that is, if you are to keep the encounter brief—you had better have your excuses ready.

The familial excuses sound something like this:

That happens to be the one thing my wife forbids me to discuss.

You should ask my husband that question. Wait here and let me see if I can find him.

The financial:

If I don't leave now, I'll be late for my job interview.

You'll have to excuse me. I've got to run and feed the parking meter.

The medical:

Oh, oh. Oooh. Damn. Sorry about this. Aahhh. My foot's gone to sleep. Ow. Oh. I'll just get up and walk around for a bit. Oooh. . . .

I think I'm going to be sick.

The meteorological:

They say it's supposed to rain today, but so far . . . Oh no, I left my windows down. I'll be right back.

Before we continue this, have you heard the weather forecast for tomorrow? I have friends coming in from out of town and I promised to give them a call right about now to let them know what to expect.

The technological:

Sorry to interrupt, but do you hear that funny noise? Sounds like it's coming from the dishwasher. I'd better go and check. Won't be a minute.

Is it ten yet? You see, my beeper isn't working so I have to phone in every half-hour.

The calendarial:

> *Boy, you sure picked the wrong day to bring up THAT subject.*

> *Ask me that in a week's time. I'll explain why then.*

The smoke created by any of these excuses will be thick enough to cover your retreat. However, if instead of retreating you would prefer to hold your ground and force others into retreat, there are a number of conversational ploys you can use to send unwanted pests scurrying back into the woodwork.

One of the most effective ways of discouraging further conversation is to apply a sort of perverse literalism to whatever is said to you. Suppose, for instance, you are asked the question, "What do you think of Ronald Reagan?" If you want to be perversely literal about it, there is only one answer: "Thoughts." Or you may respond with a request for clarification: "Compared to what?" Not even the most devout bores have the stamina to swim for long against this kind of current.

Deafness is also a powerful deterrent. Nothing takes the steam out of a dialogue (or monologue) more quickly than having to repeat everything twice. Thus, to avoid discussing Mr. Reagan all you need do is open your side of the discussion with lines like: "Could you say that again?" . . . "I'm sorry, I'm a bit hard of hearing. If you could speak just a little louder." . . . "Ronald who?" . . . "Oh, Reagan, What about him?" . . . "What does he *think?* About what?" . . .

Or you might want to ward off the question with a display of utter confusion. "What do I think of Ronald Reagan? I don't understand the question." . . . "How can I tell whether I like him? I don't even know him." . . . "I don't know what he's doing now, so I can't say if I like it or not."

If by this time they aren't already thoroughly squelched, they soon will be. Hoarse, too.

Another valuable weapon in the war on unwanted conversations is the non sequitur. People seldom linger long in the presence of looniness. So when asked your opinion of Mr. Reagan, you might reply, "I wouldn't know, I'm on a diet." Or perhaps: "It's hard to say, I've never been married myself."

Something along those lines should be sufficient to stop the discussion in its tracks.

If a little looniness goes a long way, so does a little obscenity. Suburban types in particular are put off by detours through the scatological precincts of the language. Therefore if you are lacking the inspiration to talk nonsense, talk dirty: "Reagan? I'll say one thing for him, the cocksucker has balls. Not like that little cunt that came before him, with his shit-eating grin and that fuck-up of a brother and . . ." You could go on like this awhile, but it should hardly be necessary.

When it comes to aborting awkward or boring conversations over the telephone, you have at your command the same range of excuses and stratagems given above, plus a few extra.

There is, to begin with, that important phone call you've been anxiously awaiting, or that important appointment you were just rushing out the door to go to. Then there is the household emergency, any of a thousand, most of them involving children, that demands your urgent attention. And, somewhat less theatrical but no less effective, there is the sudden, insistent summons of a ringing doorbell or a buzzing oven timer.

Perhaps the simplest excuse for getting off the telephone is the telephone itself. As soon as you realize that the conversation is about to take a turn for the worse, so does the connection: "Can you hear me all right? I can just barely hear *you*." . . . "Maybe if you speak up." . . . "What?" . . . "Yes, a little better." . . . "I'm sorry, I missed that last bit. This damned phone. It's been like this all week. Look, why don't you hang up and try calling me back?" And of course when they call back a bad connection will have become a disconnection. But, if you are unwilling to expend even minimal energy silencing the voice at the other end, there remains the ultimate in conversation-stoppers: the self-pulled plug. There is positively no comeback for this. At least not one you can hear.

*EXCUSES YOU SHOULD NEVER USE FOR
GETTING OUT OF AWKWARD OR BORING
CONVERSATIONS*
. . . and the reasons why

You wouldn't be interested in what I think.
This may well be true, but by saying so you have forced them to prove otherwise.

Can't we discuss it some other time?
Do you need to be told what the answer will be?

You wouldn't like what I have to say.
Probably not, but now you've made them eager for the opportunity to dislike it.

I'm too embarrassed to talk about it.
If you want to intensify their curiosity, this is the way to go about it.

I'm not very well-informed on the subject.
That's exactly what they're hoping, because they mean to inform you.

. . . *Unwelcome Assignments at Work*

Excusing yourself from unwelcome assignments at work is especially tricky because it requires that you maintain a delicate balance between your desire to avoid work and your desire for continued gainful employment. Any excuse that gets you out of work but also *puts* you out of work cannot be counted an unqualified success. Therefore, because your boss is interested in you primarily in terms of your contribution to his balance sheet, the best excuses will be those that show you have the company's best interests at heart.

For this reason most familial excuses are risky, as they raise a question about where your true loyalties lie—at home or in the office. Dustin Hoffman discovered this in *Kramer vs. Kramer* when he dashed off to tend to his sick child once too often and soon found himself looking for a job. So it's wise to keep your family out of your office excuses unless they can be used in a way that's good for business. Such as:

> *Damn, I was expecting it to be a slow day, so I offered to take my kid and* [your best client's] *kid to a game. I thought it might be a good public relations move, if you know what I mean* [wink, wink].

When making a financial excuse, it should always be the company's money, not your own, that you're trying to save:

> *You know, I've been looking into the costs on this job, and I've come to the conclusion that we could significantly enhance our profit position, without any loss of quality, if we*

*streamlined production to eliminate some of the unnecessary
aspects.*

By no coincidence, the plan would call for your share of the work to be
streamlined out of existence.

Medical excuses are generally safe and effective, provided they are used
sparingly and are for the most part work-related (or, better still, overwork-
related). You have a suspected ulcer from brooding over a troublesome account; you herniated yourself helping someone move a filing cabinet; you
received a mild concussion when your car hit that telephone pole as you
were driving home late after work. (Remember, though, that unlike the excuses you use to get out of domestic chores, chronic maladies are to be
avoided, lest your employer start calculating what you will cost him in future
time lost.)

All things considered, the best excuse is one that combines concern for
the health of someone else in the office with your continuing concern for
corporate health:

> *There'd be no problem if I could do the job all by myself, but
> I'm worried about my secretary. She's at the point of
> exhaustion as it is, and I'm afraid that if I give her any more to
> do right now she'll collapse just when we really need her on
> that next project.*

For a meteorological excuse to be convincing, obviously, it must pertain
to an outdoor assignment that will be adversely affected by the weather. You
can't just sit there and moan that rainy days and Sundays make you blue.
Too, the excuse should in some way relate to the company's finances. For
example:

> *My only hesitation is that in this weather the traffic will be
> horrendous, and I'd feel guilty using up valuable company
> time sitting parked in a traffic jam. Whereas if THEY could be
> persuaded to come to US ...*

Even the technological excuse—*something broke*—should be linked
somehow to your ongoing crusade against waste and inefficiency:

> *I don't mind in the least staying late to make the extra copies
> you need. I'd happily stay all night if I thought the copier*

> *would function properly for once—because then I could re-do*
> *all the jobs that it's ruined in the last couple of weeks. Do you*
> *have any idea how much we'd save by hiring somebody to do*
> *nothing but run off copies and make sure that the machine is*
> *always in good working order?*

While the calendarial excuse takes many credible forms—you are spending the morning in pious observance of one of your church's highest holy days; you are spending the afternoon shopping in order to honor a customer's birthday—it is still advisable to make your unavailability for work a form of service to the firm:

> *Well, actually, on Tuesdays I attend a management skills*
> *seminar. I haven't mentioned it before because I was hoping*
> *you'd notice the improvement in my efficiency without my*
> *saying anything. You know, I didn't want you to feel that you*
> *HAD to comment on my performance just because I was*
> *paying to improve it out of my own pocket. Ah well, my*
> *secret's out now. . . .*

All-purpose excuses—those involving blanket negatives—are, without exception, extremely hazardous to your employment and should be used only when you work for yourself and the threat of tiresome labor comes from the outside. Then, and only then, can you say, "I don't . . ." "I won't . . ." "I never . . ." Indeed, when you're your own boss you can even go on to enumerate the things you don't and won't and never do, as the late author and critic Edmund Wilson did when he had this notice printed for immediate dispatch to those who would presume to add to his work:

EDMUND WILSON REGRETS THAT IT IS IMPOSSIBLE
    FOR HIM TO:
READ MANUSCRIPTS,
WRITE ARTICLES OR BOOKS TO ORDER,
WRITE FOREWORDS OR INTRODUCTIONS,
MAKE STATEMENTS FOR PUBLICITY PURPOSES,
DO ANY KIND OF EDITORIAL WORK,
JUDGE LITERARY CONTESTS,
GIVE INTERVIEWS,
CONDUCT EDUCATIONAL COURSES,

DELIVER LECTURES,
GIVE TALKS OR MAKE SPEECHES,
BROADCAST OR APPEAR ON TELEVISION,
TAKE PART IN WRITERS' CONGRESSES,
ANSWER QUESTIONNAIRES,
CONTRIBUTE TO OR TAKE PART IN SYMPOSIUMS OR "PANELS"
    OF ANY KIND,
CONTRIBUTE MANUSCRIPTS FOR SALE,
DONATE COPIES OF HIS BOOKS TO LIBRARIES,
ALLOW HIS NAME TO BE USED ON LETTERHEADS,
SUPPLY PERSONAL INFORMATION ABOUT HIMSELF,
SUPPLY PHOTOGRAPHS OF HIMSELF,
SUPPLY OPINIONS ON LITERARY OR OTHER SUBJECTS.

In fact, contrary to the last line of his "regrets," Mr. Wilson has supplied us with an unequivocal opinion on a lot of subjects, and in the process has left us with a model of how to fortify yourself against people who wonder if you could find the time to do just one little job for them.

There are, it must be said, some jobs that it will be impossible or at least imprudent for you to get out of via an excuse. In these instances the trick is to accept responsibility (and therefore credit) for the job while getting someone else to do the actual work. Now, if you are in an office where the activities of the employees are fairly closely monitored, it would be advisable to gently prepare your boss for the sight of a colleague laboring over your assignment:

> *Are you sure this won't make Joe jealous? I mean, he sort of considers this his exclusive territory. Maybe I should just mention that I'm working on it in case he wants to be involved.*

Thus you have not only paved the way for your unsuspecting colleague to end up with the lion's share of the work, but you have also impressed your boss with your political sensitivity and concern for office morale. Another technique is to impress him with your commitment to quality:

> *If you don't mind, I'd like to bring Joe in on this if he's not too*

*busy. He's so good at this kind of thing that I know it would
benefit from his participation.*

Then, having got the green light to approach Joe, or even if you haven't
mentioned Joe's name at all, you go to Joe with the good news:

*The boss must have a lot more faith in you than he does in
me. He promised over a month ago that he would put me in
charge of this project, but now he says that you're better
qualified to handle it. He even wants me to watch you work
on it so I can see how it's done.*

The boss, of course, will think you're supervising when he sees you standing around contemplating Joe's industry.

But what if Joe is too clever to buy the flattery and the work that comes
with it? Well, you can always say that the boss wants *us* to handle the job:
Joe will look after one part of it, the hard part, while "all the rest" will be up
to you. Or you can break down the job into several parts and distribute them
among those below you in the company hierarchy. One of the nice things
about the competitive atmosphere in most offices is that the farther down
the food chain you get, the greater the appetite for challenging assignments.

Finally, you can pre-shrink the chance of getting an unwelcome job by
contriving to look busy whenever you sniff a potential job walking toward
your desk. And you can reinforce the impression that you already have more
than you can handle by being at your desk at unexpected times.

If, for example, your boss makes it a practice to come to work early, you
should occasionally show up even earlier; if he tends to work late, stay late
every once in a while. This tactic works especially well at times when one of
your associates will be conspicuous by his absence. Thus, when you know
that somebody is going to come in late, or leave early, perhaps because he
has to take his kid to the doctor, that's when you should make a point of
coming in early or leaving late, because it enables you to draw a subtle (and
highly favorable) contrast between your devotion to duty and that of your
absent colleague:

*Yes sir, it IS a bit early for me, but I knew that Joe had to take
his kid to the doctor this morning, and what with all the work*

*we have to get finished I thought I'd try to get a head start to
take some of the pressure off later when he does get here.*

And if Joe happens to be a bitter rival, you can make the contrast work to
his further disadvantage by reflecting softly:

Poor old Joe. His kid's always getting sick at the worst times.

Before going this far, however, consider the possible consequences: If Joe
gets fired, who's going to do your work for you? That's something to think
about.

EXCUSES YOU SHOULD NEVER USE FOR GETTING OUT OF UNWELCOME ASSIGNMENTS AT WORK
. . . and the reasons why

I'm too busy.
You won't be for long if you say things like this.

I don't know how.
What difference does that make? Even a brain surgeon is entitled to make mistakes.

That's too heavy for me to carry.
You don't know that until you try. So try. *Then* fall over in agony.

I don't have the right tools with me.
Don't worry, they can be provided.

Why do I have to do everything around here?
Because you've been making bad excuses like these, that's why.

. . . *Unwelcome Encounters of a Close Kind*

Declining intimacy with others, be it of the soft- or hard-core variety, is an exceptionally delicate matter, because it amounts to refusing an honor. After all, anyone who expresses a desire for more intimate association with you is paying a compliment to your attractiveness. And since it is a compliment you may well deserve by reason of your actions, if not your natural seductiveness, you must resist it only with the most extreme tact unless you want to place the rest of the relationship in jeopardy.

This requires, first and foremost, that your excuses in no way reflect on the other person. Which means that your timing will be almost as crucial as your tact, because however tactful your excuse may be for, say, not going to bed with someone, it will sound hollow if you delay using it until after you see what the person looks like undressed. So if you are to maintain a credible deterrent against unwanted sexual advances, you have to be prepared to use it as soon as you see the whites of their eyes. You can't wait until you see something else.

Moreover, it's not enough merely to persuade the other person that your reason for not having sex, or whatever, is operative regardless of who happens to be involved; you must convince your admirer that it is operative *despite* the fact that he or she is involved. Hence the traditional familial excuse—"But I'm married"—will be transformed thus:

> *Believe me, if the integrity of my marriage weren't so*
> *important to me, I would have dragged you off to bed long ago.*

Look, if I thought there was one chance in a million that we could do it without damaging my marriage, I'd gladly take that chance.

The financial excuse, too, will have a new twist:

I must tell you, and I know this will sound dreadfully old-fashioned, but I will only sleep with a woman if I'm prepared to marry her. I'm not saying that the prospect of marriage is a necessary precondition for intimacy, but the POSSIBILITY of marriage is. And, frankly, given the present state of my finances, I can't even pretend that marriage is a possibility.

You've spent so much money on me tonight—taking me to the theater, to dinner—that I'd feel like a whore if I went to bed with you now. And I want our lovemaking to be something spontaneous and beautiful, not just a quid pro quo. That would cheapen it. I wouldn't say this to anybody else, I'd be afraid that they would laugh at me, but you're so sensitive I know you'll understand.

The medical excuses, of course, concentrate the mind so wonderfully that the personal touch is hardly necessary. Whose ardor would not be quenched upon learning that your genitalia lie at the crossroads of every known social disease? Still, you may want to go with the excuse that allows you to stroke the ego even as you refuse to stroke anything else:

The truth is I went off the pill this month just to see if I would notice any difference, so I could easily get pregnant. But that's not the real reason. The real reason is that if I got pregnant I know I would never get an abortion, because it would be YOUR baby. It would be something special, something WE made together, a living reminder of our love, and that's not the sort of thing I want to leave to chance. Do you?

All right, I'll tell you. For the past couple of days whenever I've gone to the bathroom I've felt this burning sensation. I mean, it's no big deal. It's happened before and I've had sex and nothing ever happened. But with you, well, I just don't want to take any chances. I couldn't live with myself if I thought I'd given YOU something.

When it comes to meteorological excuses, the rain falls mainly on the plain girls and boys—which is why you should keep the weather out of it, unless it's already in it:

I didn't say yes OR no. What you heard was my teeth chattering.

At a moment like this—with the thunder and lightning and all—I wish you would just hold me.

Even the standard technological excuse can be perverted—sorry, converted—to account for your otherwise unaccountable lack of lust:

You want to know what's bothering me? It's the walls in this apartment. They're made of cardboard. The neighbors can hear everything that's going on. I know, I know what you're going to say. Has that ever stopped me before? No, to be honest, it hasn't. But then I've never been here with YOU before, and—I don't quite know how to say this—I don't want something I consider precious to satisfy the prurient curiosity of strangers.

Actually, I'm GLAD your car broke down out here in the middle of nowhere. You know why? Because now I'll finally have the perfect comeback for all my frustrated, dirty-minded friends who have been telling me that I was a fool for going out with you, that all you wanted was an opportunity to get in my pants. Now I can tell them what a gentleman you really are—AND what a genius at fixing things. They'll be so jealous.

With such an abundance of good excuses to choose from, it's unlikely that you will need to consult a calendar. But if you do:

It's too soon. It's been only two months since I broke up with

> my boyfriend, and if I were to go to bed with you now I would
> never know—and, more important, YOU would never know—
> if it was just a rebound sort of thing, a consolation prize. You
> wouldn't want that. You're too good for that.

> It's a point of honor. I made a solemn pledge to myself that I
> would abstain from all sexual activity until the New Year. You
> may think that's funny, but if you do you would be just like
> those people who laughed at Lovelace when he wrote, "I
> could not love thee, dear, so much, loved I not honor more."
> It's the same with me. Without my sense of honor, however
> silly it seems, I wouldn't be worthy of you.

Needless to say, this is also a perfect area for the employment of all-purpose excuses:

> I never go to bed with a man on the first date. In fact, I usually
> don't even kiss on the first date, but you're different.

> I make it a rule not to fool around with married women.

> On principle, I refuse to let sex complicate a valuable
> friendship.

But what if you have already let sex complicate a relationship, and now your partner wants to structure your intimacy, either through marriage or living together?

Your family can come to the rescue:

> It would make my child more disturbed and insecure than he
> is already.

Then there is the turn of the financial screw:

> I would forfeit my inheritance. My father said he would cut me
> out of his will if I ever married a Jew/Catholic/Protestant/
> German/Puerto Rican/black.

Assuming that your liaison has not been distinguished by celibacy, you will have burned most of your medical bridges by now, but there are still a couple that offer a way out:

I know how much you want children, so let's wait and see if I can have my vasectomy reversed.

I'm just one of those people who have to be alone most of the time. In fact, my analyst says that if it weren't for the time I spend alone, I wouldn't be able to appreciate the time I spend with you.

There is no known meteorological excuse for not getting married or living together. There *is* a technological excuse, but it's about as thin as the walls of your apartment:

You know I have to keep this apartment for another two years—and it just isn't built for two people.

The calendarial excuse is much more convincing:

Oh no, I made that mistake before. This time I'm going to wait twelve months before making a permanent commitment. It's only fair to you.

But the most concise, and most conclusive, way of avoiding a long-term entanglement is to borrow the all-purpose motto of the Jewish Defense League:

NEVER AGAIN!

*EXCUSES YOU SHOULD NEVER USE FOR GETTING
OUT OF UNWELCOME ENCOUNTERS
OF A CLOSE KIND*
. . . and the reasons why

I can't, I'm a virgin.
There's a first time for everything.

I don't know you well enough.
Then how better to get acquainted? Besides, you don't know
Warren Beatty either, but you wouldn't tell *him* that.

I'm ashamed of my body.
Which you probably should be, but by declaring it you leave
yourself open to the absurd claim that you are loved for your
mind.

I don't want you to see my underwear.
Risky, very risky. Ever heard of fetishism?

I would, but I don't trust myself.
This is just possibly the world's greatest turn-on.

. . . Suspicions of Infidelity

In theory, of course, there is no reason why we—allegedly the most intelligent form of life on this planet—should not be able to indulge in a little extramarital hanky-panky without immediately arousing our partners' suspicions. In practice, though, whenever we wander from the straight and narrow we leave behind a set of footprints that any imbecile could follow.

This is because in our zeal to hide the tiniest physical evidence (including such traditional yet essentially harmless clues as lipstick on the collar or an unfamiliar garment on the floor of the car) we tend to overlook behavioral evidence that is all but blinding to our mates.

To take just a few examples, a husband or wife would have to be semi-comatose to fail to notice when:

> —you start coming home late from work more often than before, and later;
> —you are bouncier than usual, even to the point of humming to yourself;
> —you have a lot of bad luck answering the telephone: every other time you pick it up it's a wrong number;
> —you sometimes talk in low monosyllables when on the telephone;
> —you rush to be the one to get the mail;
> —you leave for business meetings in a cloud of cologne or perfume;
> —your secretary gives your spouse long, sympathetic looks whenever he or she comes to the office;
> —you adopt a more *sportif* look in your dress;
> —you take showers at unusual times;

—you develop a sudden interest in something that previously bored
   you;
—you talk a lot about the importance of maintaining the family unit
   whatever happens;
—you get a faraway look every time a certain song comes on the
   radio;
—you are less jealous, even tolerant, of your mate's flirtatiousness;
—you buy books about the joys of "open marriage";
—you want to try something new in bed, *and you know how;*
—you ask your wife if her breasts have got smaller or something;
—you see your urologist or gynecologist twice in the same month;
—you miss your period for the first time in years;
—you start doing exercises for the first time in years;
—you get caught in a silly lie that you didn't need to tell in the first
   place.

Any two of these elements in conjunction, if they represent a significant
deviation from your usual pattern of conduct, will be enough to trigger your
mate's alarm system. Three or more constitute a web of circumstantial evidence from which you will be able to extricate yourself only if you have your
wits—and some good excuses—about you.

At the same time, when it comes to establishing your innocence of any
illicit romance you do have two things going for you. One is the fact that
unless you have blundered dreadfully (a situation that will be dealt with in a
later chapter), the evidence against you *is* only circumstantial. It doesn't
implicate you directly in any misconduct; it just seems incriminating because your mate couldn't think of any other explanation. Happily, you can.
Moreover, and this is the second thing in your favor, your mate wants to
believe your explanation—and almost certainly will, provided that you give it
in a tone of voice that clearly conveys the extent to which you are hurt and
dismayed that anyone could even conceive of questioning your faithfulness.

Thus the familial excuses will march to the beat of honor wrongly
impugned:

*Yes, as a matter of fact, I AM trying to look younger. That's
exactly why I bought a new wardrobe. It all started with*

something my son said. You know, out of the mouths of babes and all that. Well, one day he asked me why his friends' parents all seemed younger than I did. I told him that your own parents always seem older than other adults when you're growing up. But then I started thinking: Maybe he's right. Maybe I do look older. And if that embarrasses him, maybe it embarrasses you. Maybe YOU would like to see me look a bit younger. I guess I was wrong. . . .

You're absolutely right. I never DID like doing exercises. I still don't. But every time I see your mother she tells me how tired I look, as if you might be a widow any day now. Anyway, I finally decided that she might be on to something, that perhaps I really wasn't in the best of shape. So I figured that I owed it to you, if not to myself, to try to get in better shape. I thought you would be pleased. . . .

Or financially speaking:

I never said I was working late at the office. I said I was working late, period. And since you brought it up, the reason I didn't say any more was that I've been doing a free-lance job to earn some extra money so that I could buy you that coat you want so much. Incidentally, that's also why I've been making sure that I was the first one to see the mail every day. I was afraid that you would see the check come in, which would spoil the surprise. Of course, now you've spoiled it anyway. . . .

Did I REALLY go to those meetings reeking of cologne? Damn, I wish you'd said something at the time, Maybe THAT'S why . . . I suppose you might as well know. Those "meetings" were in fact job interviews. You see, for weeks now there have been rumors around the office that a lot of people are going to be let go in the near future. Nobody knows who, or when, so to be on the safe side I thought I'd start looking around. But I didn't want to say anything because I knew it would just worry you.

On the medical front, I would prescribe something like this:

Do you honestly believe that I confused—or even compared—your breasts with someone else's? Incredible. It so happens that I brought up the matter of their size for a very good reason: I wanted an excuse to touch them all over—in a different way, I mean—without making you wonder what I was up to. The truth is I wanted to feel for lumps. Do you know how many women your age get breast cancer every year? And do you know how many die because it wasn't detected earlier? All I was trying to do was satisfy myself that there was nothing to worry about—but without upsetting you. Boy, did I fail. Now we're both upset.

Since you're so desperate to know why I've been to the gynecologist twice recently, I'll tell you. It's because for the past few weeks whenever we've made love I've felt this sharp pain. But I knew if I said anything about it you would just think that I was trying to put you off, and then you'd feel rejected, and then you'd start making those sarcastic little remarks about our "so-called sex life." So I thought it would be easier for me and happier for you if I simply tried to get over it on my own.

Or if you want to be more literally under the weather:

When did I start taking showers as soon as I got home? By a funny coincidence, it was about when the weather started getting hot. Frankly, in this heat I can't imagine anyone but a slob NOT taking a shower every chance he gets.

You think YOU'VE been puzzled that I didn't get my period this month. What do you think I'VE been? Would you believe paranoid? Actually, I spoke to my doctor today and he said it was nothing to be concerned about. In fact, he said I was the umpteenth woman to call this week about missing a period. Apparently there's a stationary ridge of high pressure or low pressure or SOMETHING in the atmosphere that's creating havoc with menstrual cycles. It's quite funny when you think about it. I mean, talk about an ill wind . . .

From the world of mechanical things:

Yes, dear, I know it's late. Yes, I know what time it is. Yes, I did stop off to see someone on the way home. You got all three right. Congratulations. Now would you be interested to know whom I stopped off to see? A mechanic. That's right, I have this thing about mechanics. Only this time I HAD to see one because about halfway home the car died on me, and then died again, and again, so I took it in to be looked at. I knew that you needed the car in the morning and I wanted to make sure that it was all right. I also knew that if I phoned and said the car was in the garage you would assume that it was my fault—you always do—and then you would have started in on me the way you did when I got home. God, I wish now that I had just got the car home any old way and left it for you to deal with.

But I DID phone. Didn't your friend tell you? . . . Okay, maybe "friend" is the wrong word. After all, he denied even knowing you. . . . I think you DO know what I'm talking about. I'm talking about the man who answered the phone earlier. . . . Oh Christ, you don't suppose I dialed the wrong number, do you? Oh, that IS funny. And to think that I stayed out late just to avoid some awkward scene. . . .

And, finally, from the calendar:

Sure, I've been feeling bouncy lately. I always do at this time of the year. You DO know what date is coming up, don't you? Oh well, I guess it's more important to me than it is to you, but it's the anniversary of our first _____.

(FILL IN THE BLANK)

All right, I WAS lying. I didn't go to see my accountant yesterday, or last week either. I must say, it never occurred to

*me that you would feel it necessary to spy on me—but since
you did, now I have to tell you what I was really doing. I was
trying to organize a special surprise birthday party for you.
And it was going to be some party, too. What a pity. But we
can still do something special, just the two of us. And
besides, now you know what a poor liar I am. I could never
sneak anything past YOU. . . .*

Now, the alert reader will have noted that all these excuses, with the
exception of the meteorological ones, carry the same underlying message: *I
did it for you.* This is an important tactical point, because whenever you are
confronted by a suspicious mate your chances of successfully erasing the
suspicions will be greatly enhanced if you can link the excuse to an activity
undertaken for the benefit of the person who's suspicious. So remember:
Whatever you did, or say you did, *you did it for them.*

There may, however, come a time when you have been so totally careless about covering your tracks that no combination of categorical excuses
will save you. In these circumstances, you will have little choice but to resort to an all-purpose excuse. And, as it happens, there is one ideally suited
to such a situation. It is a sophisticated variation on the venerable play-
ground retort: *It takes one to know one.* But for it to be effective it must be
delivered in a self-deprecating, even sheepish manner:

*Actually, I have a confession to make. All this time I thought
YOU were having an affair, so I pretended to be having one
just to force your hand. I wasn't trying to get even or anything
like that. I just thought that I had probably become less
attractive, less interesting to you, and that if I started acting
secretively or suspiciously it would give me a little added
glamour and mystery—maybe not much, but enough that you
wouldn't feel any need to fool around. You know all those
times I went out and then came back late with some stupid
excuse? Want to know where I really went? I went across the
street and waited to see if YOU would go somewhere. Can you
imagine a mature, sane adult doing something like that? Can
you imagine what an idiot I felt like when I walked back*

through the door? It's so ridiculous being suspicious, such a silly waste of time. We should make a promise right now that we'll never again be suspicious of one another.

That's what is known as taking out a married-life insurance policy. It won't cover your more egregious indiscretions, of course, but it will protect you should you ever have another minor accident involving your credibility.

EXCUSES YOU SHOULD NEVER USE FOR GETTING OUT OF SUSPICIONS OF INFIDELITY
. . . and the reasons why

I know what you're thinking, but . . .
No, wrong. What they're thinking should be the farthest thing from your mind. How else can you be shocked and indignant when they reveal their suspicions?

I don't even find him/her particularly attractive.
Oh, and if you did would it be different?

I couldn't do anything now anyway.
See above, substituting "could" for "did."

I didn't know you were going to wait up for me.
See above again.

I don't have to account to you for my actions.
Yes you do. Read this *whole* chapter over again.

. . . *Entertaining the Kids*

Not surprisingly, the basic strategy for getting out of entertaining the kids is similar in many respects to the strategy for avoiding domestic chores, because the two activities themselves are so similar. (Indeed, many would argue that entertaining the kids *is* a domestic chore.) But there are two important differences. In the first place, because most requests to entertain the kids come from the kids themselves, you have the advantage of dealing with a more gullible audience. You can get them to swallow excuses that would leave grown-ups choked with laughter. And in the second place you have at your fingertips an "Off" button—*I said no, and that's final*—which if used with grown-ups would only hurt your cause, but with children only hurts their feelings.

As it is with domestic chores, the familial excuse is somewhat circumscribed by the fact that the family is the enemy. Still, there are ways of getting behind the enemy lines:

> *You promised your mother that you would clean up your room. So for once it's time to do something for HER, after all that she does for YOU. Maybe SHE would like to sit down and play something for a change. Ever thought of that?*

> *I tell you what. I'll play with you if first you go and write that letter to your grandfather that you keep putting off. He's been so good to you, and you know how he loves to hear all about the things you've been doing. So if you want me to play you'll run along and write the letter.*

Don't worry, by the way, about framing your excuse in terms of a deal. To my knowledge, a deal like this has never been accepted by a child.

Since most children have difficulty making the connection between the quantity of paper on your desk and the quantity of food they eat, it is generally futile to point to your desk-top and make groaning noises about work coming before play. Therefore your financial excuses should focus on hard cash:

> *Do you know how much I spend every year to pay for your school? Do you have any idea what it will cost me to send you to college? The least you could do is spend some time on your homework instead of always wanting to goof off.*

> *Okay, I'll take you—on condition that you pay for yourself out of your allowance. I'm not being stingy, I'm just trying to teach you the value of money. If you don't learn now to save for the things you want, then you'll end up like those poor people we saw on television.*

As a means of avoiding unnecessary exertion on your part, the medical excuses are usually reliable because the one thing that kids understand is pain. And they grasp even more quickly the idea of pain when it's related to the activity for which they want you:

> *You know I can't run on this knee. I don't know why you even bother to ask me. It's been like this ever since I was in school and we were in the championship game and I was returning a punt for a touchdown—I told you about this—and just when I got to the goal line this guy hits me from the side. I still scored the touchdown, but for a while they thought I'd never walk again. That's why I have to be so careful. One wrong move and I could be a cripple.*

> *Obviously you've forgotten what happened the last time I took you there. You were in bed for days with a cold AND an earache. Remember how terrible you felt? I was really worried about you. You don't want to take a chance on getting sick like that again, do you? Anyway, I'M certainly not going to take a chance on it.*

The meteorological excuses, while never wholly convincing to the juvenile mentality, do have occasional usefulness, depending on the prevailing conditions:

> *You must be joking. It's one big mud puddle out there. I'd get my clothes filthy if we tried to play in THAT.*

> *It's much too beautiful a day to sit around indoors playing Monopoly. You ought to be outside having fun with the other kids.*

The effectiveness of technological excuses is notably diminished by the willingness of children to play with anything, however malfunctioning or in need of repair, but excuses of this type can still be employed to good effect if pronounced with authority:

> *I refuse to play with that game until we have it fixed. It's probably just that the batteries are low, but whatever it is I'm not going to risk ruining it.*

> *There's not enough air in the ball. And not only is it bad for the ball to kick it when it's like that, it's bad for you as a kicker. You won't learn how to kick it properly if it's not blown up.*

Another category that can be drawn upon for spot duty is the calendarial:

> *Do we have to go through all this again? Don't you know by now that I always keep this time for reading/taking a walk/taking a nap? It's the only time of the week I have for myself.*

> *I can't. It's closed today.*

Obviously, these categorical excuses have all been designed for use on children. With people your own size you will have to modify the excuses to take into account the fact that grown-ups have a longer attention span and are more prone to attacks of cynicism. Fortunately, though, there is an all-purpose excuse you can use whenever your spouse is the one who proposes some appalling recreational activity with the kids: *You disapprove.* It's not a matter of taste or preference, it's a matter of policy. You are simply bowing before the parental imperative to do what you think is best for your child:

> *Actually, I've been looking forward to seeing the movie myself. I just don't think it's suitable for children.*

> *I have nothing against electronic games per se. If I did, I wouldn't have bought one for him. But I think that at this stage of his life it's more important for him to learn to enjoy reading.*

> *Of course I don't mind playing ball with him. It's fun for me, too. What I DO mind is that playing ball is the ONLY thing he wants to do. For most kids it's just another pastime, for him it's an obsession. And I think we should start to curb it now. Do you want him to grow up to be a jock?*

> *I'd love to take her to the museum—when she's old enough to appreciate it. At this age she'd be bored by most of it, understandably, and then in later years she would associate museums with boredom. That would be tragic. THAT'S what I'm afraid of.*

I mentioned earlier the strategic parallel between the techniques for getting out of domestic chores and those for making yourself unavailable to entertain the kids. Nowhere is this parallel more striking than in the most basic technique of all: avoiding the necessity to make an excuse in the first place. For example, you have to learn to recognize the early warning signs of danger. An approaching child carrying a bat and glove represents no less a threat to your happiness than an approaching spouse carrying a mop and bucket. And with both the tactic is the same: Cut them off at the pass. Busy yourself with something that absolutely precludes another activity. Or at least, in the case of children, be prepared to suggest an alternative to the activity that burns brightly in their beady little eyes.

This alternative activity should be introduced thus:

> *Ah, THERE you are. I was just going to look for you. You*
> *know, I had an idea that you might be looking for something*
> *to do. . . .*

After that, you don't have to worry about coming up with a really attractive diversion. They will be so relieved that you weren't thinking of something for them to do that might resemble work, and so happy to get away before you *do*, that they will instantly forget what it was they were going to ask you.

But suppose you have kids who are too reckless or too stupid to play it safe, who are willing to gamble against the odds in order to disturb your peace? Don't fret, all is not lost. They can always be bought. Now, in principle I am opposed to outright bribery, but when you're bribing children the sums involved are so insignificant that one must view such transactions in purely economic terms. And there is no doubt that a candy bar in exchange for a good nap is an excellent bargain.

Nevertheless, there will be those times when you simply cannot dodge being drafted to play with the kids. With child care, as with domestic chores, you can't expect to maintain a perfect record of absenteeism. But you *can* play with the kids in such a way as to make your future participation in their entertainment not avidly sought. The key, once again, is the cultivation of incompetence.

For instance, if you are conscripted to play Scrabble, put down non-words like *shrdlu*. If you're playing chess, concede after the first move. If you're playing catch, wave helplessly as the ball sails past you, and follow by retrieving it v-e-r-y s-l-o-w-l-y. Then throw it into the bushes, or over the fence. And when your playmates finally succumb to paralytic frustration, make it worse by paying fatuous homage to their skills: "I guess you're just too good for me."

Occasionally, though rarely, one comes across a diminutive pervert who actually enjoys humiliating you at games. Should you be burdened with one of these, you have but one course open to you: ruthless annihilation. Whenever and whatever you play with them, give them a fearful trouncing. Take no prisoners. Show no mercy. Make them cry.

Then gloat.

EXCUSES YOU SHOULD NEVER USE FOR GETTING OUT OF ENTERTAINING THE KIDS
. . . and the reasons why

I played with you yesterday.
You think they remember yesterday? You think they care?

I'll play with you tomorrow.
Now *that* they will remember. Kids hoard such careless declarations like promissory notes.

When I was a kid, I was expected to amuse myself.
Even if true, what does that have to do with anything?

That movie's too gruesome. It would only frighten you.
Are you kidding? That's why they want to see it.

That's no fun.
Okay, so let's hear what you think *is* fun. This should be good.

. . . *Talking to Salesmen*

Once upon a time all you had to fear from the doorbell ringing was that it might be the paper boy wanting you to pay up or the Fuller Brush man wanting to show you a wondrous new tool for cleaning your toilet bowl. Alas, times have changed. Now your doorstep swarms with Avon ladies, Amway people, Girl Scouts selling cookies, underprivileged youths selling magazine subscriptions, encyclopedia salesmen, people collecting for charity, people collecting signatures to ban the bomb or save the whales, Mormons, Jehovah's Witnesses, Jews for Jesus, and a whole tribe of others, all of them bent on peddling *something*—a product, a service, an idea, a cause.

How to disperse these pests? Short of installing a moat and drawbridge, which most people find impracticable, or installing a large, ill-tempered animal, which most people find inhospitable, the best way to get rid of those who would invade your privacy is not to open the door to them in the first place. That way you don't even need an excuse. All you need to say, once you have determined the purpose of their mission, is: "Sorry, I'm not interested." Whereupon your signal suddenly begins to fade into the deep, silent recesses of the unseen world behind your closed door. Not even the most persistent salesman will talk to a door that doesn't answer back.

However, unless you have grown up in a city like New York, where you are constantly reminded of the wisdom of not opening doors to strangers, and unless your spouse and offspring have been well rehearsed in the technique of saying good-bye to invisible people they haven't met, you will sooner or later find yourself alone in the doorway, squinting into the sunlight, while some silhouette a few inches away blats into your face, "Hi, my name is . . ."

That's when you need an excuse.

The familial excuse is ideal in this sort of situation because it allows you to appoint a family member, who of course happens to be away at the moment, as the sole purchasing agent for the household:

> *You'd have to speak to my husband—he takes care of all that.*
> *And he's not home today.*

> *I'm afraid I can't help you. I'm just a guest—you know,*
> *house-sitting for them until they get back.*

With financial excuses you have to be a little more careful, because people who solicit door-to-door are experts at dealing with pleas of poverty. You don't have enough money to contribute to charity? Then you of all people should understand what it's like for those who are even worse off than you are. You can't afford to subscribe to another magazine? That's precisely why you need this one, because it will save you money. You don't have any cash on you? We'll take a check. And so forth. Thus your excuse for failing to reward their presence on the premises should be not that it is financially difficult for you, but financially ridiculous:

> *I've already contributed twice to your organization, on*
> *condition that nobody bothered me at home. Do you want me*
> *to demand my money back?*

> *Actually, I get all the magazines I want for free, through my*
> *job. Sorry.*

Medical excuses are effective, by and large, because part of the basic training of most sales infantries is the importance of not penetrating territory already occupied by germs. Nonetheless, it is wise to warn them that they have reached the outskirts of a fever swamp:

> *Yes? Oh, I thought you were the doctor. We have an*
> *emergency here. Look, if you don't know how to control*
> *someone in the violent stages of delirium, I'd get out of here*
> *fast if I were you.*

*Before we go any further, can I ask you a question? Do you
have a lot of health insurance? Because if not, you're in
trouble. We have two cases of smallpox here. Didn't you see
the quarantine notice?*

And then there's the weather. Frankly, the weather won't help you
much, unless you are the beneficiary of divine intervention whereby a lightning bolt descends from the skies and ignites the cerebellum of the unlucky
creature blocking your doorway.

The technological excuse, on the other hand, does have possibilities:

*I bought one of those last year and it never worked. I'm still
thinking about suing the guy who sold it to me.*

According to Consumer Reports, *that's made with an
ingredient that causes cancer in rats. You mean they didn't
tell you?*

The calendarial category, while weaker than the others, can still be
amusing as a change of pace:

*You're just a day too late. I pay all my bills on the 13th, which
means that as of today my bank account has exactly zero
dollars in it. Try me again next month.*

*I take it you're unaware of the fact that Zoroastrians aren't
allowed to handle money on Saturdays?*

Less fun but more reliable are the all-purpose excuses:

I CAN'T . . . use cosmetics in my condition.

*I DON'T . . . read magazines or encyclopedias or anything
else.*

I NEVER . . . make a donation to a charity I've never heard of.

*I REFUSE . . . to support an organization that ignores the
plight of the Kurds.*

Still, even if you're armed with the best of excuses, you have to be constantly on your guard, because among the armies of mercenaries camped outside your door there will be a few commandos who have been specially trained to sneak past your perimeter defenses. They are usually camouflaged as real people, and they know not to say things like, "I represent the XYZ Company and I wonder if I could have a few minutes of your time. . . ." Instead they flash a humanoid smile and purr, "Are *you* Mr. Carroll? I thought you must be. You see, we're conducting a survey among all the most influential people in this community, and I'd be grateful if you would be good enough to give us your opinion on a few matters of current interest."

Watch it. The only opinion they're interested in is whether you would prefer to pay for the encyclopedias in a lump sum or in installments.

If you are a kind soul, you will apologize for the fact that you are a moron and don't have an opinion on anything, thus sparing them the indignity of having their subterfuge exposed. On the other hand, if you are like me, you will invite them in, make them coffee, ask the neighbors over, promise to be absolutely honest and forthcoming in your answers, offer to provide paper if they want to take extra notes, ask if they are comfortable, mention how glad you are that somebody really respects your opinion, mention how sad you were to have those people arrested last week for trespassing when they got into the house under false pretenses to try to sell encyclopedias, say that you're ready to start any time they are, admit that you may need a lot of time to think about the philosophical issues about which you feel deeply. . . . And then watch them squirm as, slowly, slowly, they are hoist with their own petard.

Equally gratifying, when the legions of mercantilism lay siege to your door, is the Boston Strangler strategy. This strategy is named after the eponymous hero of several homicides and at least one joke. I'm unfamiliar with the details of the homicides, but the joke goes like this:

> MAN (*responding to doorbell*): Who is it?
> VOICE (*responding to man*): The Boston Strangler.
> MAN (*responding to circumstances*): Darling, it's for you.

Now, in case you missed it, the strategy embedded in this slab of drollery is to leave the Uninvited nonplussed by the innocence of the Uninitiated. Or to put it another way: Whenever a huckster launches a spiel across your threshold, quickly excuse yourself and summon the nearest child. When the child materializes, whisper words to the effect that it could be worth a large increase in allowance if the clown at the door can be kept talking for another five minutes before he gets demoralized and leaves.

It's costly, I know. It's time-consuming. But it's worth it.

EXCUSES YOU SHOULD NEVER USE FOR GETTING OUT OF TALKING TO SALESMEN
. . . and the reasons why

I can't really afford to buy anything, but I'll just have a look at what you've got. . . .
And you'll see, my, what big teeth they've got.

With these kids to deal with, I'd have to have four hands before I could talk to you.
And you have only two, and the salesman has two, and he can put two and two together, and you're in for a long, long talk.

I don't need any cookies.
Does anybody *need* cookies?

How many times do I have to tell you that I don't want any?
That depends. How many times are you willing to ask?

I hate you punks coming here and trying to con me into buying this stuff.
You'll hate it worse when they come back and torch the house.

. . . Giving Presents

Unlike the other situations we have discussed so far, gift-giving is a lifetime occupation. People who want to bore you, or who want to burden you with work, or who want to drag you off to bed, or who want to sell you something—these people come and go. But people who want presents from you will *always* be there. Therefore if you are to have any prospect of fending them off without at the same time offending them, you must make them understand that they cannot expect presents, nor do you expect presents from them.

Accordingly, I am going to dispense with the categorical excuses altogether in this chapter and go straight to the one all-purpose excuse:

> *I never give presents, and I never expect presents from*
> *anyone.*

Of course you can't just leave it at that. You owe them some sort of an explanation, unless you're willing to be compared unfavorably to Scrooge every time someone you know has a birthday or gets married or looks under the Christmas tree. And, as it happens, there are three very good reasons why you should forswear the giving of presents.

To begin with, a "present" is a present only to the person to whom you gave money when you bought it. That's why merchants get together every so often and invent a Mother's Day or a Father's Day or some other Day on which you can celebrate your purchasing power. *You* are the only present worth giving: your friendship, your loyalty, your high esteem. A purchased present is nothing more than "just a token," as the old familiar phrase so aptly has it. Why, then, give tokens when you can give the real thing?

Secondly, giving a present is a symbolic, and therefore hazardous, way of rendering an opinion about the person on whom you bestow your largesse. When people say sweetly, insincerely, "It's the thought that matters," they are closer to the truth than they know. Because a gift shows, in a material way, what you think of someone; it is an approximate metaphor for your idea of that person's wants, needs, tastes, priorities. That's why you should stifle the urge to give a gift. Approximate metaphors are dangerous. They have a way of blowing up in your face.

Thirdly, every present comes with a string (if not a rope) attached, a string that represents the tug of reciprocity. By giving a present you are signaling your willingness, if not your eagerness, to accept one in return. You haven't discharged an obligation so much as you have created one. You have set up a coaxial exchange system, one that can never be broken without unfortunate consequences for the relationship. It is far better to maintain a dialogue of words than of things. Not only are they cheaper, but they last longer.

* * * * *

Of all the presents you can give, easily the most perilous for any friendship is the temporary present that calls itself a loan. Loans are simply presents that you have to return. What's more, you are expected to return them in the same condition in which you received them—which is, of course, impossible. Any house that you borrowed will show traces of your having lived in it. Any car you borrowed will bear the signs of added mileage, if only on the odometer. Even the money you borrowed, unless it is given back instantly, will have its edges nibbled away by inflation and its ink faded by the loss of interest it could have been earning.

Worse yet, you are not only expected to return these temporary presents in the same condition in which they were given to you by your friends, but you are expected to hand them over in the same condition in which your friends *remember* them.

Thus, while they will fail to notice that the house is twice as clean as they left it, they will suddenly spot the wine stain on the carpet which has been there as long as they have, or the half-empty bottle of orange juice in the refrigerator, or the frying pan you put back in the wrong cabinet, or the alarm clock on which you changed the setting, causing them to be late for work. Nor will they appreciate the fact that you had the car washed and filled with gas before returning it; they will notice only the little scratch on the side that they never noticed before, or the cigarette butt you left in the ashtray, or the strange station to which you tuned the radio, or the way you readjusted the rear-view mirror, almost causing them to have a fatal collision.

And that's if all goes well. If it doesn't, and it seldom does, you might as well write off the friendship that the loan was intended to honor. Never mind that you were unable to repay the money on time because you lost your job and your child had to have an operation: If that happened to be the time your friends saw a new sailboat they wanted to buy, or an attractive investment they wanted to make, they will forever resent you for having their money when they needed it. No matter that their teenage son had already burned the tread off the car's tires pretending he was Mario Andretti: They will only remember that their precious car was in an accident (due to a blowout) when *you* were driving it.

No matter that the house they gave you for a month was a ticking time-bomb—the heating element in the oven should have been replaced long ago, the plant in the living room was diseased when they bought it, water from the bathroom had been seeping through the upstairs floorboards for years, vandalism had long been a problem in the neighborhood, the television set was an antique, and burglars had been watching the house ever since your friends forgot to cancel the newspaper and milk deliveries before you moved in. No matter. They will only take note of the fact that it was while *you* were in residence that the oven exploded, the plant died, a huge stain appeared on the kitchen ceiling, a brick flew through the living room window, the TV expired, and burglars ransacked the house (probably while you were out having their car fixed).

Nor will they have the grace to say, upon their return, "You poor dear, what you must have been through" or "Thank God you were here to take care of things." No, instead they will say, through clenched jaws, something like: "Well, this isn't quite what we expected to find" or "You were right, dear, we shouldn't have gone away." And if they really hate you they will try to disguise the fact with bitter little attempts at humor: "Oh well, I suppose it could have been worse. It might almost be worth going away again just to find out how it could have been worse." Or: "It looks like you didn't get out much. I see the rest of the town is still standing." Or: "Why don't these things ever happen to that old bitch across the street? Say, you wouldn't like to look after *her* house for a while, would you?"

I speak from some experience in these matters. Although I have never had a house or a car or a large sum of money totally self-destruct while in my custody, and thus I have never fallen into total ignominy, I do know what it's like to surrender custody of something with the words, "Oh, there are a couple of things I ought to mention. . . ."

Once, when I was between marriages, a kind and well-meaning friend offered me the use of his splendid house and his equally splendid Porsche while he was away on vacation. Even though I knew better, I accepted. And since I knew better, I made it a point to resist driving the Porsche and to restrict my activities inside the house to those essential to the feeding of his cat and his guest, in that order. Nevertheless, on the day before he returned, the cat, for reasons known only to her, decided to die. Panicked by this turn of events, I decided that I'd better take the Porsche around the block so that at least my friend's car and his cat wouldn't both be dead on his arrival. You know the rest: I had backed the car barely ten yards down the driveway when the transmission fell out. Thus, despite superhuman efforts on my part, my friend returned to find two of his most prized possessions lying extremely still.

I should perhaps add that he was gracious enough to accept my explanation without question. He even made a wan attempt to laugh it off. But I could see in his face that *deep down* he knew I had stripped the gears while chasing the cat up and down the driveway in a deranged but successful attempt to scare it to death.

The moral: Never give your house or your car or your money to anyone, even for a day. Even for an hour. They will only hate you for it later. Which will be nothing compared to the way you will feel about them.

* * * * *

There is, it should be said, one present—but only one—that is always worth giving: the present you give to the tall, dark stranger in the night who places the tip of a metallic object among your lower vertebrae and suggests a hasty benefaction. This person is unlikely to be interested in your theories about the harmful effects of gift-giving. Indeed, it is quite likely that he will be moved to demonstrate for you some of the harmful effects of *not* making a donation to him under the circumstances.

For unexpected occasions such as this, you might consider carrying with you a specially-prepared present—a second wallet—just in case you are suddenly called upon to make a mandatory gift. This second, sacrificial wallet should contain the following:

> —a pocket calendar for a bygone year;
> —a snapshot of a former lover;
> —a few expired credit cards;
> —a number of out-of-date membership cards or other types of identification bearing your old address;
> —a couple of blank checks on an account you've closed;
> —a promising quantity of cash, consisting of all singles, with a sprinkling of Polish zlotys and Argentine pesos and funny money with Richard Nixon's portrait on it.

This is the perfect present for the aggressively needy. For not only will it create joy in their hearts when they first contemplate its contents, but upon later inspection their eyes will fill with tears when they realize that you have given them a gift beyond compare—the priceless gift of humor.

EXCUSES YOU SHOULD NEVER USE FOR GETTING OUT OF GIVING PRESENTS
. . . and the reasons why

Why should I? They didn't give me anything for MY birthday.
So you're willing to admit that you *do* believe presents are for bartering?

It will only spoil him.
Isn't that the idea?

I'm still looking for just the right thing.
Now, of course, they're dying to see what you consider "just the right thing"—and if you ever find it they probably *will* die.

You won't tell me what you really need.
They need you to stop asking.

I thought I'd wait to see what everyone else got you.
Do you wait to see what everyone else says before you speak to them?

. . . Looking for a Job

There is no doubt about it: Job-hunting is the most degrading, dispiriting, enervating, tormenting, forlorn activity ever devised by man. For sheer torture, it ranks alongside watching the Chicago Cubs play baseball or translating Alexander Haig into English. But whereas the Cubs afflict only a tiny minority of sports fans, and Mr. Haig is required listening only for connoisseurs of brain damage, job-hunting is an integral part of the human condition.

Even so, it wouldn't be quite so tragic if there were a cure for it that didn't produce appalling side-effects. But since the only "successful" cure is permanent employment—i.e., having to get up early every morning and go to work for somebody—most independent thinkers and freedom-fighters would prefer simply to ease the symptoms of the disease for as long as possible in hopes that some day soon either modern science or modern warfare will make employment obsolete.

It would be nice to be able to say that that day is at hand, that we can now look forward to a world where jobs—and the pain of looking for them—have been stamped out. But I cannot. The pro-work lobby remains as powerful and implacable as ever, and as determined as ever to promote the further proliferation of jobs, whatever the ultimate cost in human suffering.

This doesn't mean that there is no reason for hope; indeed, so long as Detroit continues to turn out cars that remind us of the horrors that jobs can produce, there will be growing pressure on legislators to recognize that even the most primitive jobs, if made widely available, pose a serious threat to everything we sit for: life, liberty, and the pursuit of idleness.

However, until something is done to halt the spread of jobs, there is nothing much you can do but relax, take it easy, and contemplate the variety of excuses you can use to avoid looking for one.

The familial excuses will concentrate on the good of the family as your top priority:

> *Sure, I could find a job tomorrow if I wanted to. No problem. But I think it would be a terrible mistake. For the family's sake I want to be selective and wait for the right job—not just any job—to come along. Remember, it's not only MY job, it's OUR job, because you can't help bringing part of it home with you. And I've seen too many families and marriages suffer because somebody felt forced to take the wrong job.*

> *If there's one thing I've learned from this experience, it's the importance of having time to spend with the kids. For the first time I feel like a real parent. But I've also learned a lot from them—they've given me a sense of perspective, a vision of the future, that has changed my whole way of thinking about jobs and work. I now realize that the time I spend with them is more valuable than the money I could make working.*

Since presumably your finances have been the main casualty of your unwillingness to seek employment, the financial excuses will require a certain deftness of touch:

> *Do you seriously want me to see somebody about a job with my hair looking like this? I'd be more likely to get arrested than hired. No, I'll have to get a haircut first. And I can't afford to do that until the unemployment check comes in.*

> *My accountant says that in the long run I'd be better off starting a business at home rather than looking for a job. It's more profitable, and you get all sorts of tax breaks. So I've ordered a couple of books on the subject and I'm going to look into it seriously.*

Almost any medical excuse is serviceable in this situation, including those that focus on the state of your emotional health:

> You know what my real problem is? I'm pathologically shy when it comes to asking somebody for a job. I stammer and shuffle my feet and look at the floor, and by the time I've finished I can tell the guy is wondering if I'll be able to get home all right. I'm really going to have to try to conquer that before I talk to any more people.

> It would be an exercise in pure masochism to look for a job right now considering the shape I'm in. Don't you think they can see that I don't have any self-confidence? Do you think anyone wants to hire a manic-depressive? If I approached anyone about a job now all I would do is ruin any chance I might have of getting the job later on when my confidence is back.

The meteorological excuses, as usual, are very specific in their applicability:

> I am NOT lazing about. I just want to look my best for my job interviews. That's why I need to get a suntan.

> I can't today. I let the kids take my umbrella.

The technological excuses should revolve around damage to your job-seeking paraphernalia:

> I can't go out and meet anybody until the cleaners fix the hole they put in my suit. Of course, they're claiming they didn't do it. . . .

> The answering machine isn't working properly. I already know of two important messages I've missed just in the last couple of days, and I hate to think how many others there might have been. So I can't afford to leave the telephone for a minute.

The calendarial excuses go something like this:

> *According to my horoscope, this is the worst possible time for me to look for a job. Don't laugh, I'm serious. It may be mumbo-jumbo, but it's never been wrong about this sort of thing in the past.*

> *There's no point in looking for a job this month—everyone's on vacation.*

And here is an all-purpose excuse which can be used either in conjunction with one of the categorical excuses or as a rejoinder to those who would question the sincerity of the other excuses:

> *I AM looking for a job. You know, looking for a job isn't like looking for Easter eggs. It's a matter of putting together resumés, collecting references, putting the word out among friends, writing letters, making phone calls, WAITING for phone calls. . . . If you had even the slightest idea how many phone calls I've made only to be told over and over again that there is no need for my services, I don't think you would be quite so cruel about reminding me that I'm not exactly in demand these days. Is it MY fault that everybody thinks I'm overqualified? Do you think I LIKE sitting around the house all day doing nothing?*

Finally, there are a couple of things you should know about being self-unemployed. If you keep these in mind they will help you to prolong your idleness and at the same time discourage those near and dear to you from harboring unworthy suspicions about your talent for leisure.

First of all, you must recognize that your success in avoiding the likelihood of employment creates the potential for resentment among those members of your family who work for a living. Consequently, you must be careful not to be observed conspicuously enjoying the fruits of your non-labor. This means, for example, that even if you have a perfect record for getting out of domestic chores, your heightened visibility around the house together with your lowered contribution to the family exchequer obliges you to perform certain duties that in the past would have brought forth a blizzard of excuses. Any household job will do, but the best is the one that your spouse most detests. It is hard to be annoyed at the indolence of others when they have just done a job that you hate doing yourself.

Another tip: Never be curled up comfortably in bed when your mate leaves for work. It doesn't matter that you were up late playing cards, or watching a late movie on TV, or that it will be several hours before you achieve full consciousness. *Get out of bed!* Draw on whatever resources you have to create the impression of energy and eagerness to meet the challenges of the day. Not until you hear the door close should you go back to bed and resume sleeping. Likewise, however fresh and rested you feel at the end of the day, and you *should* feel great, the moment you hear the door open you should adopt a haunted and desolate look, as if you barely survived being crushed by the burden of your inactivity.

Then fix a drink to cheer yourself up.

EXCUSES YOU SHOULD NEVER USE FOR GETTING OUT OF LOOKING FOR A JOB
. . . and the reasons why

Because I might find one.
This is no time to be funny.

Work is the curse of the drinking classes.
I said this is no time to be funny.

I'll never do anything to help capitalism survive to exploit the masses.
So get a job and help guarantee its downfall.

I don't know where to look.
Have you thought of glancing at the classified ads after you've finished with the sports pages?

I'm not into the work reality, man.
Do you want to say that again, just for old times' sake?

. . . Eating the Inedible

As a brief glance at any bestseller list will confirm, there are few things on this earth we take more seriously than the preparation of food. Consequently, there are few insults more devastating than a refusal to eat the food that has been prepared for you. (I am talking about meals that are served to you in someone else's home. It is assumed that if you are in your own home or in a restaurant you are capable of making known in advance your culinary preferences as well as your gastrointestinal idiosyncracies.)

For this reason you should approach your host's dinner table as you would a minefield, knowing that one wrong move and you're in big trouble. You should also know that most categorical excuses are wrong moves. The only type of excuse that offers a safe escape from a plate full of unappetizing food is the medical one. Fortunately, though, it offers an abundance of good escape routes.

Indeed, the dinner table is the one place where an ordinary old stomach-ache will earn you a special exemption. This is because, although people hold you accountable for your taste buds, they regard your stomach as something over which you have no control. Furthermore, as your stomach is the first organ to be intimately involved with whatever you eat, people tend to take seriously its feelings in the matter. They know that if it forms a bad opinion of what you eat, the results can be extremely disagreeable for everyone present. Similarly, any malfunction of the lower digestive tract is accepted prima facie as a powerful reason for abstaining from food, no questions asked. (No questions are asked because any description of the symptoms could put others off *their* food.) Also quickly accepted are excuses based on peptic ulcers and obscure medications which are liable to produce unpredictable reactions when mixed with certain foods.

But whenever you are faced with something truly inedible, throw an allergy at it. Allergies will never fail you. However bizarre the allergy you come up with, it will never be challenged. (My young son, for example, claims to be allergic to parsley, and he even has *me* believing it.) Better still, allergies are forever. Their potency lasts for as long as you want an excuse not to eat something. If ever there was conclusive proof that it is our biological destiny as humans to make excuses, it is that we, alone among the species who inhabit this planet, invented both the telephone and the allergy.

In addition, there are two all-purpose excuses which are known to work whenever the food in front of you is an affront to the senses. The first, which is founded on your religious or philosophical principles, I cannot in good conscience recommend. You see, people don't believe in principles the way they believe in allergies. So when you say that you can't eat something because you're a Jew or a Muslim or a vegetarian or whatever, you immediately brand yourself as either quaint or boring. And in any case, if you are sincere about your principles you shouldn't be eating with people who are so insensitive, or so ignorant, as to serve you something that those principles forbid you to eat.

The second all-purpose excuse, by contrast, is one that I heartily endorse. It is simply a recitation of the fact that you never eat much of *anything*. I'm particularly fond of this excuse because in my case it happens to be true, and therefore I am aware of the special benefits it confers. Having a notoriously small appetite gives me a choice: I can either take a couple of bites and push the rest of the food around the plate, in which case my host remarks indulgently on my strange eating habits, usually employing the word "typical"; or I can eat more than is my normal custom (though still less than anyone else), in which case my host is hugely complimented. Either way I have eaten exactly what I want, in the quantity I want, without giving offense.

Obviously, however, if this excuse is to serve you as well as it does me, you must cultivate a reputation for eating only microscopic amounts of food. It's no good making a pig of yourself one day and an ascetic the next. You have to be consistent. If this imposes an intolerable strain, remember that you can always eat before you go somewhere and after you come home, as well as in between. Although this may in time create a waistline that belies your professed meager eating habits, there is a good medical excuse for that, too: You have a glandular problem. Indeed, that's *why* you eat so little.

* * * * *

I suppose it goes without saying that timing is the key to the success of any excuse involving food you don't want to eat. The best excuse, of course, is the one that is delivered before you see the food. That way there can be no suspicion that the excuse has anything to do with how the food looks (and if it looks delicious, you can always override your own veto, thereby flattering your host). The next best excuse is the one delivered after you've seen the food but before you've tasted it. And after that it's the one you give after you've tasted it but before you've gagged. And so on . . . until you finally get to the excuse just after you've thrown up.

But even if you are too courteous, or too gluttonous, to say anything about the food until your entire sensory apparatus is in open mutiny, there is still a way out. All you have to do is smack your lips and say, "My, this *is* delicious. What did you put in it?" Then, when you find out, you look longingly, disconsolately, toward the remains on your plate, intoning the words:

> *I should have known. Why is it that I'm only allergic to things I love?*

Hard to say. Could be something to do with the way they taste.

EXCUSES YOU SHOULD NEVER USE FOR
GETTING OUT OF EATING THE INEDIBLE
. . . and the reasons why

I'm not hungry.
A meal that someone makes for you is a *gift*; it's not an offer that you accept or reject depending on whether you *need* it.

I can't eat this late at night.
It's only late if you are already planning to go to bed early.

I'm dieting.
Are you willing to repeat that when the dessert comes around?

I'm too full. I stuffed myself at lunch.
And you must have used up all your charm while you were at it.

I'm sorry, but I think it's wrong to kill another living creature just to eat the flesh from its carcass. To me it's cannibalism. And when you think we could feed the world's starving millions if we gave them the grain that we now feed to animals to fatten them up before we slaughter them by crushing their skulls with sledgehammers and slitting their throats and . . .
Oh, shut up.

. . . *Visiting the Relatives*

When you need to come up with an excuse for not visiting your relatives, you start with one major advantage and one major disadvantage compared to other situations from which you want to excuse yourself. On the one hand, you have the advantage of knowing your relatives better (or at least longer) than most people, and therefore you should have a good idea as to what type of excuse is most likely to carry weight with them. As against that, however, relatives are notoriously susceptible to feelings of neglect, which causes them to be highly suspicious of any reason for not seeing them. If you fail to see friends for a few weeks, it will be taken as a sign that you are probably very busy. If you fail to see your relatives for the same period of time, it will be taken as a sign that you're deliberately boycotting them.

This is because your relatives are always convinced, despite your protestations of loyalty and affection, that you really don't care about them, that you're not in the least grateful for all they've done for you, that you're lazy and debauched, and that you'd do almost anything to get out of paying them the courtesy of a visit. They may be right, of course, but that's beside the point. The point is that any excuse you offer them will have to pass through a screen of mega-skepticism.

Consequently, as relatives consider it your *duty* to visit them, the best way of sidestepping this onerous task is by appealing to a higher duty. Thus your excuses should in some way reflect the sacrifices you're willing to make to safeguard the well-being of your immediate family.

In the familial category, the kids should always come first:

> *I wish we could make it, but we have a PTA meeting*
> *tomorrow night. Ordinarily I'd prefer to be stretched on the*

*rack than have to sit through one of those things, but this one
I feel is too important to miss. Apparently there's a serious
drug problem at the school, and I want to find out just how
bad it is in case we ought to be thinking about alternative
schools.*

*What a shame! That WOULD be the only time we have free to
take the kids shopping for clothes. They're growing so fast
that they have hardly anything that fits them anymore. They
especially need more warm clothes, with the weather
beginning to turn cooler. You haven't heard of any sales on
children's clothing, have you? We could sure use a bargain or
two right now.*

The financial category can also be called upon to furnish evidence of
your devotion to your spouse and offspring:

*We would so love to come, but I'm afraid we have a rather
crucial date with our accountant scheduled for then. He
wants to talk to us about a plan he's devised to incorporate us
so that we'll be able to put aside more money tax-free for the
kids' education and our own retirement. I'm not quite sure
how it works—but I certainly want to find out.*

*Actually, I have to go and see my bank manager tomorrow to
try to talk him into giving me a loan. The kids need a lot of
dental work done and I'm afraid that if I put it off until I can
afford to pay for it there might be permanent harm done. I just
don't want to take that chance.*

The medical category provides a particularly rich vein for mining excuses, but you have to be careful: Some relatives will seize any opportunity,
whether or not it is offered, to nurse their ailing kin back to health. So to be
on the safe side you should restrict yourself to excuses that involve infec-
tious diseases or conditions that don't respond to chicken soup and sympathy:

*Of course we'll be there—provided the doctor tells me what I
want to hear tomorrow morning. I'm hoping he'll say that I've*

simply let myself get run down from working too hard lately, and that with a couple of days' rest I'll feel my old self again. What I'm AFRAID he'll say is that it's not going to be as easy as that, because I have exactly the same symptoms as a friend of mine who came down with mononucleosis last year. So I'm keeping my fingers crossed. . . .

You'll never guess what happened. Remember how you used to take me on those nature hikes when I was little? Well, yesterday I was trying to think of something to do with the kids that they would enjoy and learn from at the same time, and all of a sudden it came to me: I'll take them on a nature hike! So I did, but it turned out to be more of a nature hop than a hike, because I sprained my ankle so badly that I'd howl if my foot even touched the ground. Today it's so swollen that I won't be going anywhere unless I can get there on my hands and knees.

From the meteorological category:

Personally, I'd love to get out of the house, but since all the rest of us are just getting over colds—or maybe I should say getting over one giant, collective cold—I don't think it would be wise for me to take them out on a day like this. Can we have a rain check?

You're right, it IS a perfect day for a visit. Unfortunately, it's also a perfect day for pollen—which means that [your husband's/wife's] hay fever is so bad that we shouldn't even have a window open, much less go outside.

From your catalogue of technological failures:

We don't dare take the car out until we get the new inspection sticker. Apparently there's something wrong with the brake lights, and until we get them fixed the car won't pass inspection. Anyway, it's not so much the chance of getting stopped that worries me—I've got two tickets already. It's the chance of getting rear-ended with the kids in the car.

Could we postpone it for just a little while? I'll tell you why. It's so rare that we have a chance to get together these days that I like to take pictures whenever we do see you. And my camera's not working properly at the moment. I don't think it's anything major, but I'd like to wait until it's repaired before we come over. You know how I hate to miss "photo opportunities"!

And, finally, from your repertoire of calendarial excuses:

Oh, you mean THIS Sunday. I thought you meant the 23rd. No, this Sunday one of my firm's best clients is coming in from out of town and I drew the job of looking after him. I suppose I COULD say that something's come up, but I don't think this is the best time to disappoint my boss.

It looks like NOBODY is going to see us for a few weeks unless we suddenly get lucky and find a place to live. You know we have to be out here by the end of the month. And that means we have to spend every spare waking moment looking for somewhere to live. In fact, if you DO see us before the end of the month it probably means that we've decided to move in with you. You think I'm joking, don't you?

Yes, but they're probably not eager to test their luck.

* * * * *

Although you will never be able, in the eyes of your relatives, to discharge satisfactorily your obligation to honor them with your presence, you can reduce that obligation by showing your willingness to visit them—at cunningly selected times. If, for example, they go to bed early, you might suggest stopping by after you've been to the theater one evening. When they are ill, offer to bring them something, coughing and sniffling a lot as you talk. If you know they are going to be out at a certain time, go around and leave a note saying how sorry you were to have missed them. If they follow a fairly set routine, drop in whenever it's likely to be most inconvenient—and then retreat quickly, apologizing profusely for the intrusion.

Still, you must face the fact that, as with domestic chores and child-entertaining, sooner or later your number (and possibly your bluff) will be called. Don't despair. Accept the invitation, or the hint, gracefully. Say what fun it will be. Say how much you're looking forward to it. Then get to work *fast* designing the last-minute emergency that will spoil your fun.

EXCUSES YOU SHOULD NEVER USE
FOR GETTING OUT OF VISITING THE RELATIVES
. . . and the reasons why

It's awkward for me because I know you don't like my husband.
Now you've done it. Now they will insist on having the chance to *prove* how much they like him, even if he *is* a lout.

My wife had her heart set on going to the beach.
Just as they thought: You'd do anything for that little tramp.

We were up until late last night at this party and today we're feeling dreadful.
So getting drunk with your sleazy friends takes precedence over seeing your family?

You know we don't eat that early.
All right, they'll starve themselves for two hours, and you can sit there listening to their stomachs growl.

We have to go to my mother-in-law's this afternoon.
Aha! You have time for *them* but not for your own flesh and blood.

. . . Paying the Bill

It is said that for everything there is a time: a time to be born, a time to die, a time to sow, a time to reap, and so forth. It's a rather naïve and deterministic view of life, to be sure, but it is nonetheless one that most of us could live with if we didn't have to live with its burdensome corollary: There is also a time to pay.

Unlike most other "times" by which we measure out our existence, times for paying are both cyclical *and* unpredictable. For not only do they come around with tedious regularity, usually at the first of the month, but they also sneak up on you when you're not expecting them—when, for example, you are happily cruising down the highway and you suddenly notice that your rear-view mirror is flashing red, or when you're relaxing after lunch in a restaurant and suddenly your companions' hands all become paralyzed the moment the check lands on the tablecloth.

These are not happy times. But neither are they times for defeatism. Defeatism is appropriate only to the time for dying, when you know that you can't be defeated *again*. The time for paying, on the other hand, is preeminently a time for making excuses. While excuses for not paying are essentially the same in form and character as all other excuses for not doing something, and may be subdivided into the same categories, your selection of the right excuse will depend to a greater degree than usual on who takes delivery of the excuse—that is, on who wants to be paid.

And what, you ask, is the difference between someone to whom you owe money and someone *else* to whom you owe money? The answer is simple: None, if you intend to pay up anyway. But if you intend to prevent your funds from being exhausted—which can only be accomplished by exhausting those with claims on your funds—you will first make the crucial distinction between individuals (i.e., people) and institutions (i.e., bunches of people).

The distinguishing characteristics of individuals are:

> —a tendency to call you up at odd hours;
> —a sense of urgency, sometimes bordering on desperation;
> —an eagerness to receive payment in full;
> —a tendency to give up after a while, and eventually to forget about it.

By contrast, the distinguishing characteristics of institutions are:
> —a tendency to write you letters;
> —a knack for giving *you* a sense of urgency;
> —a willingness to accept partial payment if tied to a schedule of further payments;
> —a dogged refusal to forget about it.

Thus it can be seen that the two different types of would-be payees require different types of excuses. Moreover, the excuses will often benefit from different means of delivery. For example, whereas excuses involving individuals are best delivered orally, institutions as a rule are best dealt with by mail, lots of mail, all kinds of mail—excuses, explanations, requests for explanations, small checks that keep the computers busy, change-of-address notices, anything that adds to the wall of paper between you and them.

Anyway, when the moment of reckoning arrives, there are the familial excuses:

> *This is really embarrassing. It seems that my wife has been writing checks on our joint account without telling me, and now the account's empty.*

> *My husband left me two weeks ago, and now I need every cent I've got to hire a good lawyer. Because if I don't get a generous alimony settlement I might as well give up on ever being able to pay for ANYTHING.*

Or the strictly financial excuses:

> *Let me take care of this. I assume they take Carte Blanche*
> *here, because I don't have any cash on me. . . . What a*
> *nuisance. Oh well, the next meal's on me.*

> *I don't have a dime to my name. If I did, I'd use it to call*
> *somebody who knows about declaring bankruptcy.*

Or the medical excuses:

> *Right now what little money we have is going to pay for*
> *psychiatric help for my husband. He's on the verge of a*
> *nervous breakdown because of the pressure of being in debt.*

> *I finally had to admit to myself that I was a pathological*
> *spender and that I needed professional help. So now every*
> *penny I make goes to a debt manager who gives me a regular*
> *allowance to live on and then makes all the decisions himself*
> *as to how and when my outstanding obligations should be*
> *met. I'll give him a call and tell him to put your name in the*
> *hat.*

Although there are no really convincing meteorological excuses for failing to pay up, there are two distinct kinds of technological excuses. The first concerns your unwillingness to pay:

> *I have absolutely no intention of paying for something that*
> *breaks down a week after I got it. And I'm certainly not going*
> *to waste my time and money sending it back to you. If you*
> *want it you can come and get it. But you ought to be too*
> *ashamed to want to see the sort of thing you're trying to foist*
> *on the American consumer. I've a good mind to report you to*
> *the Better Business Bureau.*

> *I'll pay the rent just as soon as the heating works properly, the*
> *light in the hallway is fixed, and the radiators stop clanging at*
> *night. Not before.*

The other kind of technological excuse involves breakdowns affecting your ability to pay:

> *But I sent you a money order weeks ago. Are you SURE you haven't received it? Please go back and check again. It's such a hassle to get it replaced. As little faith as I have in the Post Office, I can't help feeling that it must have reached you but somehow got misplaced or credited to the wrong account or something.*

> *That wretched bank of mine takes forever to credit my account with checks I've deposited. Sometimes they can take two weeks or even longer. Anyway, I've got the money; it's just a matter of waiting for the checks to clear. I guess there's nothing we can do but be patient.*

The calendarial excuses might include:

> *I was so disgusted with my last bank that I switched to another bank. Of course that means it will be two or three weeks before my new checks arrive.*

> *I'm afraid I'm at the mercy of my own customers. They're always a month late in paying, which makes ME late. What can you do?*

What indeed?

EXCUSES YOU SHOULD NEVER USE FOR GETTING OUT OF PAYING THE BILL
. . . and the reasons why

I'm a little short at the moment. The cab fare was a lot more than I expected.
If you were that low on cash, what were you doing taking a cab?

It's all I can do just to pay my kids' school fees.
Haven't they heard of public schools where you live?

I have a liquidity problem.
Does that mean you're broke, or do you just need to go to the bathroom?

I made a couple of bad investments recently.
That's what people *always* say when they've just come back from the track.

I'm waiting for my ship to come in.
What are the rest of us supposed to do? Gather at the pier?

PART TWO

GETTING OUT OF TROUBLE FOR . . .

. . . Wrecking the Car

Of all the things for which you can get into trouble, there are many more serious than wrecking a car. But there are few, if any, that involve so many people for you to get into trouble *with*. There is the driver (or, God forbid, the pedestrian) you hit, and there is the owner of the car you were driving (presuming you had borrowed it), and there is the policeman who comes to the scene of the accident, and there is the insurance company, and the person on whose hedge the car finally came to rest, and the spouse who always fretted about your competence behind the wheel, and the parent who always nagged you about having "one for the road," and the boss who will be annoyed by your decreased mobility and increased tardiness. And, if you're really unlucky, others.

Obviously, no one excuse is going to satisfy *all* of these vultures, so you will have to do some careful picking and choosing, and perhaps some blending, to get precisely the right excuse for that person whose curiosity represents the greatest threat at any given time.

The place to begin this selection process is the technological category— that is, with some version of "The Car Did It":

> *The brakes failed just as I reached the bottom of the hill. If I hadn't swerved when I did, I hate to think what would have happened.*

> *The steering wheel locked as I went into the turn. Thank God there were only two people waiting to cross the street. Otherwise it could have been a massacre.*

> *How was I to know the windshield wipers were defective? Of*
> *course I realized it as soon as I switched them on, but by then*
> *it was too late. I couldn't see a thing.*

To put these excuses into reverse, so to speak, you can offer a rendition of "The *Other* Car Did It":

> *I thought it was against the law to drive without brake lights.*
> *All I can say is the guy's damned lucky that I have quick*
> *reflexes or he wouldn't even BE here to moan about his*
> *"whiplash."*

> *Maybe when he wakes up he'll understand why they tell you*
> *to dim your headlights when you see another car approaching.*
> *The jerk.*

The familial excuses, on the other hand, should only be used when there is a high statistical probability that you can get away with an utterly irrelevant explanation. For example, statistics show that the police have the highest divorce rate of any occupation, and that four out of five people get mad as hell when their spouses come home late without the car they drove away in. Thus:

> *It was really MY fault, officer. You see, normally I have split-*
> *second reactions—I mean, nine times out of ten I could have*
> *gotten out of the way of that fellow when I realized he wasn't*
> *going to move—but ever since my wife told me this morning*
> *that she was divorcing me I haven't been very good at keeping*
> *my mind on what I'm doing. I don't know why I'm telling you*
> *this. There's no reason why you should care. After all, you*
> *probably have a wife who understands the pressures of your*
> *job and is happy to put up with them. Not me. This will just*
> *convince her that she's right to leave me.*

> *Darling, I was in such a frantic rush to get home so you*
> *wouldn't be angry with me that I turned into the wrong*
> *driveway—well, ALMOST into the wrong driveway—and*
> *there was this tree . . .*

Like the familial excuses, the financial excuses avoid addressing the proximate cause of the accident:

> *It wouldn't have happened if I hadn't been so concerned about getting to work on time. It was my first day in a new job and I wanted to make a good impression. Well, I certainly made an impression.*

> *I was so busy rehearsing what I was going to say at my job interview that I didn't notice the lady backing out. I still had the presence of mind to get out of her way, but unfortunately that put me in somebody else's way.*

The medical excuses:

> *All of a sudden I got a cramp in my right leg. The pain was unbelievable. I couldn't move my foot off the accelerator.*

> *The doctor didn't warn me that the cough medicine would make me so woozy. I could barely get my eyes in focus. Say, what's IN that stuff?*

The meteorological excuses:

> *You'd think they would put up some kind of warning when the roads are icy and dangerous like that.*

> *The sun hit the back window of the car in front of me and for a moment I was blinded by the glare.*

The calendarial excuses:

> *I should have known better than to drive near the campus on a Saturday night.*

> *I suppose I was due for an accident. After all, I'd driven for twenty-five years without getting so much as a scratch, and you can't defy the law of averages forever.*

In addition, there are two excellent all-purpose excuses for the erratic behavior of your car leading up to the accident. With the first one, which I have already discussed in the introduction, you blame everything on the intervention of dogs traveling at such high speed that it is no wonder that nobody else remembers seeing them. This excuse is best reserved for accidents that occur at night, or in conditions of poor visibility, when nobody could be expected to see a fast-moving hound. The other excuse is that you were chasing a hit-and-run driver who had bowled over an old man several blocks back. God knows, you were only trying to be a good citizen.

A word of caution, however: If at the time of your misadventure you have recently consumed libations on a scale frowned upon by the constabulary, don't try to give any excuse. Do as little talking (and walking) as possible. In fact, the best course is to seat yourself quickly near the remains of your vehicle, and then stare silently into space, as if in shock. When asked to explain what happened, shake your head slowly and sigh, "I wish I knew. It all happened so fast."

I myself can vouch for the efficacy of this tactic. Once, after a most convivial luncheon in Hollywood, I was driving along Sunset Boulevard when suddenly I performed a maneuver the point of which eludes me to this day. I made a left turn in the middle of a block, at least thirty yards away from the nearest cross street. As a result, I put myself abruptly in contact with a car full of Mexican gentlemen coming in the opposite direction. After being pried out of my now hopelessly disfigured little MG, and after checking to make sure that I hadn't done any damage to the people in the other car, I limped to the curb and followed the script outlined above. It worked like a charm. Police and spectators alike bathed me in sympathy. Later, of course, I had to come up with something a little more edifying, and a little less histrionic, for the insurance company.

Speaking of insurance companies, *they* know a delightful excuse when they see one. That's because they see so many. Indeed, since every automobile insurance claim must be accompanied by an explanation of the events that necessitated the claim, insurance companies are undoubtedly the world's greatest repositories of wonderful excuses. Here is a small sample of excuses that people have actually given to their insurance companies to account for their misfortunes behind the wheel:

—My accident was due to the road bending.

—I bumped into a lamppost which was obscured by human beings.

—The other car collided with mine without giving warning of its intentions.

—A pedestrian hit me and went under my car.

—I ran into a stationary tree coming in the other direction.

—An invisible car came out of nowhere, struck my vehicle, and vanished.

—The pedestrian had no idea which direction to run, so I ran over him.

—My car was legally parked as it backed into the other vehicle.

—As I approached the intersection, a stop sign suddenly appeared in a place where no stop sign has ever appeared before. I was unable to stop in time to avoid an accident.

—The guy was all over the road. I had to swerve a number of times before I hit him.

—The accident was due to the other fellow narrowly missing me.

—To avoid hitting the bumper of the car in front, I struck the pedestrian.

—The telephone pole was approaching fast. I was attempting to swerve out of its path when it struck my front end.

—I pulled away from the side of the road, glanced at my mother-in-law, and headed over the embankment.

—I knocked over a man. He admitted it was his fault, as he had been knocked down before.

—To avoid a collision I ran into the truck.

—The accident was caused by me waving to the man I hit last week.

I offer these solely for your amusement. If you think you might try one of them some day, I have only one bit of advice for you: Please drive carefully.

EXCUSES YOU SHOULD NEVER USE
FOR WRECKING THE CAR
. . . and the reasons why

It could happen to anyone.
How many other smashed-up cars did you see being towed away?

The guy wouldn't move over and let me pass.
Sounds like he knew what he was doing.

I had the radio turned up, so I couldn't hear the siren.
Did you have your blindfold on, too?

I was trying to keep my eye on the idiot behind me.
. . . leaving nobody to watch out for the idiot in front of him.

It was time we got a new car anyway.
What do you do when it's time to move? Blow up the house?

. . . *Being Late for an Appointment*

As anthropologists are fond of noting, our more backward brethren never cease to be amused by the fact that we in the "civilized" world walk around with small metal machines strapped to our wrists to help us distinguish the present from the past and future. Now, if they think that's funny, imagine what their reaction would be if they knew that despite the sophisticated gadgetry to which we manacle ourselves we still manage to be late as often as not.

When the laughter died down, they would undoubtedly begin to wonder how we explain this curious phenomenon. That's when we would reveal the secret of our superiority: *We have excuses.* We didn't become civilized for nothing.

Because there are few experiences more tiresome than the non-experience of waiting for someone who is late, the best excuses for keeping people waiting are those that portray you as a co-victim. They were kept waiting only because *you* were kept waiting. And you're none too happy about it.

Hence the excuses with a familial ring:

> *I would have been here much earlier if my car had been available for the purpose for which it was designed. However, I must tell you that my wife's already uneasy relationship with the internal combustion engine reached an all-time low today. She contrived to run out of gas. Now please don't ask me how a grown woman with perfectly good eyesight can drive around for hours without ONCE noticing the fuel gauge in front of her face. Or maybe she did. Maybe she thought the "E" stands for "Engorged." God knows. I'll ask her if I ever go home again.*

I come before you as living, if not livid, proof that "they also serve who only stand and wait." As a service to my aged, arthritic grandmother I thought I would pick her up at the airport this morning and drive her into town. Little did I know that she intended to dismantle her house and bring it with her. I've never seen so much luggage in my life. In fact, I was beginning to think I never WOULD see it all: When she left she must have checked her bags at twenty-minute intervals, because that's the way they arrived on the conveyor belt.

The financial excuses:

Remember that fellow I told you about who's owed me money for the past two years? Well, guess what? He phoned last night and asked if he could come around today and give me the money. Guess what else? He didn't come. I suppose he figured that after waiting two years the shock of repayment might be too much for me.

Can somebody please tell me why banks bother to install ten tellers' windows when everybody knows they only intend to put tellers behind two of them? For that matter, can anybody explain to me why the shortest line always moves the slowest? Or why people over 60 and under 5'2" are never able to cash a check or make a deposit in less than ten minutes? You don't have to answer now, but the next time I'm late I'd appreciate it if you would consider these matters in my absence, and also pray for my return.

The medical excuses:

I've come here straight from the doctor's office. No, I lie. I've come straight from the doctor's waiting room. It seems that the doctor was called away to perform emergency surgery, probably on a sand trap, and his nurse was good enough to inform me of this before I'd even finished reading last year's copies of People *magazine.*

Now I KNOW times are bad. When you go to have your teeth cleaned, and your dentist sends you next door to a dental hygienist, who brings in a radiologist, who refers you to a periodontist across the hall, who suggests you see the orthodontist down the corridor, who sends you back to have your teeth cleaned, I mean you KNOW the economy is worse off than your teeth are. Jesus. What time is it anyway?

As all but the most extreme meteorological conditions can be anticipated, and thus allowed for in your planning, they should seldom be cited as reasons for your lack of punctuality. The same goes for technological excuses involving breakdowns in public transportation. Public transportation is *expected* to break down, and therefore the prudent person is expected to make the necessary allowances in his schedule. There are, however, problems with machines that cannot reasonably be anticipated:

Anybody want to buy a car battery cheap? I know where you can find one. Wait, I take that back. I know where you CAN'T find one—in my car. When I got in the car to come here, I put the key in the ignition and, you know, I found out for the first time what they mean when they talk about the sound of one hand clapping. That's exactly what it sounded like. Some bastard stole my battery.

While you should take every precaution against being late for an appointment, tardiness in itself is a relatively minor offense, a misdemeanor in the statute books of decorum. To keep people waiting, on the other hand, is a major felony. So whenever you think you are going to be late you should phone in an interim excuse to prevent a crime against the clock from becoming a crime against humanity. All you need say is, "I'm going to be late. Don't wait for me. I'll explain when I get there."

That's enough. As you said yourself, you can explain when you get there.

EXCUSES YOU SHOULD NEVER USE FOR
BEING LATE FOR AN APPOINTMENT
. . . and the reasons why

I've never seen anything like the traffic out there.
Yes you have. So have they. Every day.

I couldn't find a taxi in the rain.
Nobody above the mental age of eight would *try* to find a taxi in the rain.

My watch must have stopped.
How clever of you to have noticed.

My bus was late.
Of course it was. The only bus that was never late is now in the Smithsonian.

I didn't expect you to be here right on the dot.
You mean you thought they were like *you?*

. . . *Failing to Show Up*

The number of usable excuses for failing to show up is sharply limited by the fact that such excuses have to do double duty, because you are in double trouble: first for not showing up, and second for not calling up to say you couldn't make it. Therefore, whatever you claim it was that kept you away from your appointment will have to be something that also kept you away from a telephone.

It will have to be something, in other words, that rendered you insensible and/or incommunicado. You were knocked out, or locked up, or kidnaped, or arrested, or hijacked, or hospitalized, or in some other way cruelly victimized by fate. Whichever calamity you choose will then be grafted on to one of the categorical excuses to give it added resonance. Thus, for example, you were not merely hospitalized for the period of time during which you were expected elsewhere, but you were hospitalized for observation after collapsing from exhaustion as a result of working yourself into the ground to earn extra money to be able to send your kids to summer camp, and your brother who took you to the hospital was supposed to telephone and cancel your appointments but he must have forgotten in the stress of the moment.

Even a semi-discretionary form of insensibility, such as sleeping, can be used to account for your absence if it is built into a categorical excuse. There is, for instance, the unconsciousness that derives from familial circumstances:

> *I was up most of the night with my kid. He had one of those*
> *stomachaches that produce an eruption of bawling every hour,*

*or as soon as you get back to sleep—whichever comes first.
By the time I finally got to sleep the sky was already getting
light. But I still would have made it this morning if my
husband hadn't had an unprecedented seizure of sympathy for
me, which prompted him to look after the baby himself and let
me sleep. I don't know why he should suddenly feel sorry for
me the one morning I WANT to get up.*

And then there is the somnolence produced by financial pursuits:

*Every night this week I worked late, I even brought home
work from the office, just so I could take off early yesterday.
And what happens? I come home early, take a shower, and sit
down to relax for a little while before getting dressed to come
and see you. Well, I was so tired that I dozed off and the next
thing I knew it was after midnight. I was so angry when I
realized what had happened that I couldn't sleep the rest of
the night. So now I'm tired again. I can't win for losing.*

There are, of course, any number of medical problems capable of induc-
ing a comatose state, as well as some cures:

*Ever since my doctor made me quit drinking I've had this
terrible insomnia. I guess for all these years when I thought I
was drifting off to sleep like a normal person I was in fact
discreetly passing out. In any case, I couldn't get to sleep last
night—again—so in desperation I took a couple of sleeping
pills. Let me tell you, they work. I slept through the sunrise,
and the alarm, and for all I know an earthquake or two. By the
way, what day is this?*

Everybody's favorite technological excuse—"the alarm didn't go off"—is
a little too popular to be really convincing unless you add a personal touch:

*You know how they say a Rolls-Royce is so quiet that the only
sound you hear is the clock ticking? Well, in my bedroom this
morning about the only sound you DIDN'T hear was my
alarm clock. My wonderful new foolproof digital alarm clock.*

*Actually, it IS all those things—except foolproof, because last
night it just sat there without a murmur while my wife set the
alarm for seven o'clock in the EVENING.*

Speaking of personal touches, there is probably no other situation in
which the Ten Commandments of excuse-making are more pertinent than
that in which you seek to deflect the blame for your failure to show up.
When the people you've disappointed ask, "What happened to you?" they
don't want to hear that "something came up." They want to hear the details
of what came up, they want to hear who's responsible for what came up,
they want to hear the echoes of your frustration over what came up, they
want to hear the topical background to what came up, and they want to be
amused by what came up.

In short, they want a good story—however bizarre, however implausible. (Indeed, the more bizarre it is, the more it takes on a kind of strange
plausibility. Remember Commandment VIII regarding the Law of Inverse
Credibility?) So follow the example of the Cuban lawyer in Miami who used
his familiarity with voodoo to explain why he failed to show up for the trial of
a client: He absented himself, he said, because he had misplaced the rat's
tongue that he used to put a curse on his adversaries in court.

And just as those who were martyrs to your nonappearance are entitled
to a good excuse, they are entitled to it *soon.* If there is anything more infu-
riating than having to wait for someone who never materializes, it is having
to wait for an explanation. I can attest to that. So, too, can a former magazine editor in New York who has now apparently, and appropriately, disap-
peared without trace. (A gentleman of unprepossessing stature with a talent
to match, he had already worked his way down the mastheads of several
magazines when we first met, so I cannot claim sole credit for his subse-
quent vaporization, much as I would like to.) Anyway, the gentleman in
question invited me to lunch one Friday, and then never showed up. Finally,
after waiting at the bar for over an hour, by which time my pupils had become fatigued from contracting and dilating every time the restaurant door
opened and closed, I telephoned his office. He had left for the weekend, his
secretary informed me. When I suggested that his departure was somewhat
premature, considering that we had a lunch date, she replied that yes, well,
uh, you know, she *had* tried to telephone me the day before.

It's hard to say which I found more insulting—the bad manners or the bad excuse. At any rate, I sent the gentleman a postcard saying how sorry I was to have missed him and congratulating him on his new job. The latter sentiment, of course, was intended to detonate a little explosion of gossip among an editorial staff already seriously decimated by defections. Sure enough, it was only a matter of weeks before my erstwhile patron had been asked to vacate his place in the ranks of the employed—due in part, I am told, to questions about his loyalty—and when last heard from was at some pains to leave no doubt that he had also vacated his place in the ranks of my well-wishers. Pity. But I digress.

Odd as it may seem, the best alternative to the promptly delivered, intricately detailed excuse is the "accidental" excuse that incubates for several days before being released:

> *I was just phoning to confirm for tomorrow night. Eight*
> *o'clock, right? . . . What do you mean? . . . You're not*
> *serious. . . . No, I'm positive you said NEXT Thursday, not*
> *THIS Thursday. Here, I have it written down. I even canceled*
> *a late meeting so that I'd be sure to be there on time.*
> *Honestly. I'm not kidding. Believe me, you DID say tomorrow*
> *night. . . .*

Don't stop now. They're beginning to believe you.

EXCUSES YOU SHOULD NEVER USE
FOR FAILING TO SHOW UP
. . . and the reasons why

I wasn't feeling well.
Presumably the pain was most intense whenever you gestured toward the telephone.

I had nothing to wear.
They know. They've seen you before. But they invited you anyway.

I lost your address.
You're a real bloodhound, aren't you?

I got caught in the rain.
Caught doing what?

I forgot.
As long as you're forgetting things, forget this excuse.

... *Forgetting a Birthday or Anniversary*

People are funny about birthdays and anniversaries. What's funny is that they take them seriously. No matter that the earth has rotated on its axis about two trillion times already, or that each rotation is pretty much like the one before it; no matter that being born is the one human activity that everybody does more or less equally well, or that getting married is less complicated than getting a good cleaning lady. People still insist on commemorating that single rotation of the earth, that one day on which they began breathing on their own or stopped living alone.

Although I like to think I am indifferent to these solipsistic rituals myself, and scornful of the mythologies constructed around them, I have to admit that I do prick up my ears ever so slightly whenever I hear the date or even the year of my birth mentioned, and I tend to give my horoscope a casual glance whenever someone leaves an astrological column lying around, and I've been known to feel brief pangs—well, twinges—of something like wistfulness on the anniversaries of my former marriages.

Clearly, then, the wholly irrational importance we attach to these occasions is an index of the irrational importance we attach to ourselves. Unsure as we are of the significance of our existence, we try to establish it by the act of celebrating it. This means, among other things, that we tend to forgive those who sin against us the rest of the year so long as they are properly pious on our personal holy days. It also means that we tend not to forgive the bastards who forget.

Thus it is advisable to have ready a selection of penitential offerings, otherwise known as excuses, in the event that you fail to take note of a day that is sacred on somebody's calendar. These offerings may be made in the name of the father, or the son, or any other member of the family:

I promised your father that I would pretend to be unaware that it was your birthday. I think he had some sort of surprise planned for you. You don't suppose he forgot, do you? Oh God, he'll die. Please, for his sake, don't let on that you know. I'll have a quiet word with him about it and then in a few days we'll "surprise" you, okay? But you mustn't ever let him know that I told you.

I did NOT forget your birthday. I couldn't forget it even if I wanted to. What I couldn't remember was the exact date—I mean, which date was YOURS. I don't think I ever told you this, but everyone in my family was born in August—at least everyone I care about—and I've never been able to work out whose birthday was when, and then YOU come along and make it even more confusing. . . .

Did you honestly think that I didn't know it was our anniversary? Christ, talk about irony. I was convinced that YOU had forgotten it. In fact, my mother phoned a couple of days ago and predicted that you would forget. Well, we certainly showed HER.

Yesterday was your birthday? Damn. I lose. I had a bet with my sister that your birthday was on the 16th. She always wins. Oh well, I imagine YOUR family has better things to do than sit around arguing over when MY birthday is.

This financial excuse works well if you want pity as well as forgiveness:

Actually, I did remember. But I wasn't going to say anything until I could afford to buy you something nice.

The most apt medical excuse, if it is to be effective, should be delivered with a straight face, and preferably a long one as well:

I'm not surprised that I forgot. I've been forgetting everything lately. It seems I have what they call transient global amnesia. The doctor says it's only a temporary condition, but that doesn't make it any less frightening. Ever since I watched my grandfather going senile I've had this morbid fear of premature senility, and you know amnesia can be one of the symptoms.

Of the technological excuses, probably the best is the one that involves a failure on the part of the store where, according to you, you bought a gift to mark the occasion:

Of course I remembered. You DID get my present, didn't you? It should have been delivered ages ago.

Finally, the calendarial theme offers these variations:

You'll get a kick out of this. I was so embarrassed about forgetting your birthday last year that this year I decided not to take any chances, so I made a note in my diary a month in advance just to make sure that I left myself plenty of time to get you a gift. What happened was that I immediately went out and bought you a gift, brought it home and tucked it away in a safe place, and then forgot all about it. I tell you what, this year for MY birthday why don't you simply give me a calendar with your birthday circled in red?

I had it written down in my diary, but my diary vanished about two weeks ago and I've been living in a world of missed connections ever since.

To aid in the presentation of your excuses, it is helpful to keep on hand a number of props: greeting cards, postcards, and small gifts that you have stockpiled in advance for use whenever a birthday or anniversary takes you by surprise. With the greeting cards you simply add a note on the back of the envelope to the effect that you just found this in your desk or handbag, hence its tardiness. And with postcards you put a P.S. at the bottom—in a different pen—indicating that the thought was there on time even if the card wasn't.

Small gifts, however, remain the best guarantors of a successful excuse. By maintaining an inventory of presentable items you can always produce instant proof that you didn't forget a hallowed day in the life of another. Better still, you can usually produce instant feelings of guilt in another person for suspecting you of having forgotten.

As any practiced excuse-maker knows, that alone is worth the price of the gift.

EXCUSES YOU SHOULD NEVER USE FOR FORGETTING A BIRTHDAY OR ANNIVERSARY
. . . and the reasons why

I didn't think it was that important to you.
At least you make up in honesty what you lack in sensitivity.

I didn't think you would want to be reminded that you're a year older.
Sorry, Mr. Tactful. Wrong again.

You forgot to remind me.
They didn't forget, they just wanted to find out who their real friends were.

I had other things to think about.
Oh, that changes everything. We certainly wouldn't want your brain synapses clogged with too many thoughts, would we?

It slipped my mind.
That's understandable, considering how easy it was for all the good excuses to give your mind the slip.

. . . *Forgetting a Name*

To forget a birthday or anniversary is to demean someone's self-importance; to forget a name is to deny someone's *self.* It is a direct challenge to a person's very identity. That's why some people, usually the most forgettable, are willing to go to ridiculous lengths to give themselves (or their offspring) unusual names, or to give their ordinary names extraordinary spellings. They are hoping that by changing their labels they will make themselves distinguishable from the herd. It is a forlorn hope, of course. If people are not memorable, their names will not be remembered. And they will never forgive you for it.

To make matters worse, the very people who are marked for oblivion tend to be the same ones who come up to you and say, "Hi! Remember me?" Which makes it much harder to disguise the fact that you never thought they were worth depositing in your memory bank. Formerly, as a callow and somewhat haughty youth, I didn't bother to disguise this fact. Indeed, when people asked me if I remembered them, I derived a certain wicked pleasure from replying, "Not from the front." Or: "Not unless I have to." Or: "Hard to say. Do you have any old pictures of yourself?" Now, several years and many enemies later, I know better. Now I smile engagingly, and make excuses.

Mostly I make familial excuses:

> *You know, I have to tell you this. You remind me so much of*
> *my younger sister* [or older brother, or first wife, or favorite
> cousin, or anyone else in the family who can inspire a

passable imitation of fondness] *that whenever I see you I can only think of HER/HIS name. I hope you're not insulted. In fact, you ought to be flattered, because there's nobody in the world I love and respect more than my* [sister, brother, whoever . . .].

When we met I was so worried about my child—he was very ill at the time—that I missed your name. And then we had such a delightful and interesting chat that, frankly, I was embarrassed to admit it. It's sort of like waking up with someone you've just spent a lovely night with and suddenly realizing that you never got her name. I bet you know that feeling. . . . I THOUGHT you would.

You'll have to forgive me, but your name escapes me at the moment. You see, I just learned this afternoon that I'm pregnant, and the only names I can think of right now are names for the baby. I know it would sound silly to anyone else, but you're the sort of person who would understand.

If you prefer a financial excuse, you might consider this one:

There are two things I didn't tell you when we met. One is that I had been fired about two hours before, so I wasn't in very good shape for meeting people, to say the least. As a result—and this is the other thing I didn't tell you—when we were introduced my concentration wasn't quite what it should have been, and I didn't hear your name properly. Now that I'm employed again, will you give me another chance?

With medical excuses for your memory lapse, the obvious candidate is, once again, amnesia. A little too obvious, one could say. Try this instead:

This is going to come as a surprise to you, but I owe you an awful lot. The fact is, for years I've known that I had a drinking problem—you know, I'd go to a party and the next day I couldn't remember anything about it—but it never occurred to me that I was an alcoholic until the last time we saw each other. Because afterward I thought to myself, "What a nice man, what a marvelous conversation . . ."—and yet I couldn't remember what we talked about. I couldn't even remember your name! That's when I knew that I needed help. And I got it. Now all I need is your name and I'll feel completely rehabilitated.

In the technological category you can always put the blame on a faulty or absent hearing aid, but this can result in severe damage to your credibility if you have never been known to wear a hearing aid, and may cause permanent damage to your eardrums if the nameless ones are thus motivated to reintroduce themselves at a higher decibel level. Or you can tell them—with admirable candor, I might add—that their names were accidentally shot down during the misfiring of neurons through your cerebral cortex. With this, however, there is a sizable risk that they won't know what you're talking about, which makes it a bad excuse. And there is a tiny risk that they *will* know what you're talking about, which makes it worse. So forget it, if you'll pardon the expression.

Remember, instead, the two shrewdest ploys I know for covering up your failure to remember someone's name. The first one was invented by Tallulah Bankhead and later refined into a whole new mode of communication by Régine, heroine of various nocturnal spaces for the well-to-do with nothing-to-do. It is simply to call everybody by the same name. The name is "Darling."

The other, better ploy comes from Johnny Carson. When faced with someone whose name he should remember but doesn't, Mr. Carson says apologetically, "I'm sorry, I don't remember your name." Whereupon the other person obliges by saying, "James Woods." Carson's instant reply: "I meant your *last* name. Of course I know you're James. It was the 'Woods' I couldn't remember."

So if you have as much trouble remembering excuses as you have remembering names, just repeat to yourself this little mnemonic formula: "I can't see the Woods for the James."

EXCUSES YOU SHOULD NEVER USE FOR
FORGETTING A NAME
. . . and the reasons why

I meet so many people it's not possible to remember every-
one's name.
What are you, a census-taker?

I was close, wasn't I?
This isn't a game of horseshoes, you know.

I'm not much good with foreign names.
Unless you call yourself Running Bear or something, you
have a foreign name yourself.

But the last time I saw you, your daughter was calling you
"Ricky."
As if you couldn't tell from the funny looks his wife is giving
him, he doesn't *have* a daughter, dummy.

It's because you look just like What's-his-name.
We might as well look at the bright side: Whatever you say
from now on, you can't make things any worse.

. . . *Drinking Too Much*

Ever since early Roman times the followers of Bacchus have been a savagely persecuted minority. Preachers have denounced us, wives and husbands have threatened to leave us, neighbors have banged on our walls, strangers have accused us of saying things we don't remember saying, policemen have pulled us over to the side of the road and made us perform humiliating and unnatural acts, doctors have made disparaging remarks about our livers, politicians have levied punitive taxes on our sacramental substances, employers have threatened to fire us just because we come back from lunch happy, and our places of worship have been closed down on Sundays, the day we most need them. Yet still we endure, unbowed and unrepentant, steadfast in our faith that we were sent into the world to have a good time.

Nevertheless, in recent years we have begun to witness ugly outbreaks of anti-hedonism on an unprecedented scale. Flagrantly anti-hedonist organizations like Alcoholics Anonymous, which we once laughed off as harmless gaggles of loonies, are now allowed to operate openly and to spread their poisonous propaganda. Even trusted friends and fellow votaries can now be heard using blasphemous and provocative expressions like "Perrier" and "Sanka," well-known code words among those who recoil at the sight of people enjoying themselves.

What to do? Obviously we cannot risk an open confrontation with our tormentors. Not only would we be outnumbered, but we would probably be outwitted as well, given our tendency to get silly and laugh a lot when gathered together. Nor can we rely on guerrilla tactics, such as spiking their drinks, because it only makes them more aggressive when they realize why they're having fun.

This leaves us with but one course of action if we are to remain alive and well and living it up. It is the same course we have followed unsteadily through the centuries: the course of ducking behind the nearest excuse.

Generally speaking, medical excuses are the most versatile:

> *I think the least the doctor could have done was warn me that these pills don't mix with alcohol.*

> *I know it must look like I'm drunk, but I had a serious inner-ear infection several years ago which impaired my sense of balance. Normally I can cope with it, but sometimes when I'm tired I get this dizziness.*

> *It had nothing to do with drinking. I admit I had a couple of drinks just to steady my nerves, but I always stammer and repeat myself when I'm under stress. And if you make a big thing of it, it will only get worse.*

> *For your information, the latest medical studies show that the body NEEDS alcohol. That's why drinkers on the whole live longer than non-drinkers.*

And my personal favorite:

> *Actually, I had LESS to drink than usual. The problem is that for the past week I've cut down drastically on my drinking—at your insistence, need I remind you—and now my tolerance for alcohol is so much lower that it only takes a couple of drinks to do me in. Maybe I should start drinking more again. Would you prefer that?*

The financial category is also rich in possibilities:

> *It's always like this when I have lunch with that particular client. He just doesn't know when to quit—and he won't let anybody else quit either. Do you know when we left I still had one drink that I hadn't even touched?*

ASCII

> *I only did it for the money. I knew he would never agree to a loan if he was sober, and he would have been suspicious if I had just bought HIM drinks and not had any myself.*

> *You probably won't understand what I'm talking about, but I find that a certain amount of drinking definitely makes me more creative in my work. It's no coincidence, you know, that of the six Americans who have won the Nobel Prize for Literature, five were alcoholics. Of course, I think that's carrying things a little TOO far.*

The familial and technological categories, respectively, yield these examples:

> *I dropped by to say hello to my brother, and he fixed these delicious drinks with lime juice and coconut. Of course I should have known that he would put vodka in them.*

> *The car broke down right outside a bar. And since the bartender was kind enough to let me use his telephone to call a tow truck, I thought it was only decent to have a drink or two there while I was waiting for the car to be towed. I had no idea it would take them so long to come.*

The classic calendarial excuse needs no examples. It was a day for celebrating something, that's all. And so naturally you celebrated. Didn't everyone?

This is the one excuse for which you are allowed to look mildly post-festive. With all other types of excuses you must adopt the resigned look of the frequent victim of circumstances. This is because whatever people say to you when they accuse you of drinking too much—they can't bear to see you ruining your health, they can't bear to see you making a fool of yourself—the truth is they can't bear to see you *happy.*

So for your own sake, and the sake of future revels, be sure to kill any sign of joy yourself—before the killjoys get you.

EXCUSES YOU SHOULD NEVER USE FOR DRINKING TOO MUCH
. . . and the reasons why

What could I do? They kept refilling my glass every five minutes.

Which therefore must have been the rate at which you were emptying it.

Don't worry, I know when I've had enough.

You mean you had too much on purpose?

I was just having one for the road.

In light of the fact that 25,000 people are killed on the road every year by people who had "one for the road," you really should try to think of something else to have one for.

No one else thought I was drunk.

How on earth would *you* know?

You just don't like me to have fun.

Now you've done it. You've admitted you were having fun. Might as well go ahead and get really twisted now. It won't be as much fun as before, but with luck you'll pass out soon.

. . . Insulting the In-Laws

Let's face it: Most of the things for which we get into trouble could be avoided if we simply changed our pattern of behavior. This, however, is not the case with insulting your in-laws. It is an absolutely immutable law of nature that sooner or later, consciously or unconsciously, you will say or do something that your in-laws find insulting. It's inevitable. Indeed, the chances are very good that you have already insulted them merely by marrying your way into their midst.

I know. During my relatively short but wretchedly misspent life I have managed to accumulate no fewer than four mothers-in-law and three fathers-in-law (the fourth dropped dead, I swear, upon being told of my plans to marry his daughter), as well as three brothers-in-law and eight sisters-in-law. Eighteen in all—and at one time or another I have succeeded in insulting every single one of them. How could this be, you ask yourself, given my benign disposition and almost legendary thoughtfulness? I will endeavor to explain.

Like most rational beings, I hold these truths to be self-evident:

>—It's tacky to wear anything that an animal or a plant didn't wear first.
>—Any music that's described as "easy listening" causes impotence, and probably baldness as well.
>—Members of the pro-gun lobby should be made to walk through Harlem at night with signs reading, "I believe in every citizen's right to bear arms and I have $1,000 in cash on me."

—The Social Security system should be abandoned—if not permanently, at least until I'm 65.

—There is good wine and there is bad wine, and there is rosé.

—Anyone who voted for Richard Nixon more than once should have to undergo a memory test before being allowed to vote again; more than twice, a lobotomy.

—Health foods are bad for you.

—Chewing gum is bad for everyone near you.

—Anyone who visits a doctor twice in the same year is a hypochondriac.

—The existence of Barbra Streisand and the existence of God are mutually exclusive concepts.

—Baseball is the true sport of kings, and the Red Sox are its princes.

—The Fifth Amendment should be repealed, or at least rewritten to exclude Teamsters and Italians.

—New Jersey looks like the back of an old radio.

—Most American cars are recycled beer cans, which means the beer cans have served *two* tasteless functions.

—Restaurants with mongrelized menus (e.g., duck à *l'orange*) should be closed down.

—Ditto Chinese restaurants where you have to ask for chopsticks.

—All Irishmen have a birth defect that makes it difficult for them to tell the time or the truth.

—Sex is for fun, and a lot of sex is a lot of fun.

—Public funds should be withheld from any college or university that does not include among its degree requirements either a proficiency in Latin or a proficiency in plumbing and speedy auto repairs.

—Suburbs are for dying in, not living in.

—People who drape themselves with anything that has a designer's name splattered across it should be forcibly resettled en masse a hundred miles from the nearest shopping mall.

—Men with mustaches are of low moral character.

—Public obesity should be declared a misdemeanor; public obesity in shorts, a felony.

Now, any sane person would agree that these are hardly inflammatory beliefs, yet it is quite astonishing how they have succeeded in inflaming wave after wave of my in-laws. Which just goes to show that some people— to wit, your spouse's simple-minded relatives—will take offense at anything. It also goes to show that in these circumstances you cannot depend on the usual types of excuses.

In the first place, these are not usual circumstances. For once, it's just possible that you are not to blame for being in trouble. In the second place, you are not dealing with usual people. Whereas most people waste no time in letting you know of their displeasure at your behavior, in-laws are the last to tell you that you're in trouble with them. Instead they tell everyone else, beginning with your spouse, and leave them to deliver the message.

Consequently, when dealing with in-laws, it is necessary to frame a different type of excuse, and to deliver it in a different way—indirectly, by way of the same messenger who first brings you the news that your in-laws are in a frenzy of axe-grinding.

The excuse is that, whatever you said or did, *they misunderstood! They took it the wrong way!* You were only teasing:

> *I had no idea your father was so sensitive about his paunch. I*
> *mean, HE jokes about it. I really thought he'd be amused*
> *when I said that if he ever fell over he'd rock himself to sleep.*
> *I tease MY father like that all the time, and he enjoys it. He*
> *knows it's a sign of affection. He knows I only do it because*
> *I'm fond of him. And it's the same with YOUR father. I'd*
> *never dream of teasing him if I didn't like him so much.*

Or you were only being honest:

> *I thought they wanted my honest opinion. After all, they did*
> *ask for it. And it so happens that I DO believe the Roman*
> *Catholic Church has been responsible for more misery,*
> *suffering, poverty, ignorance, and superstition than any other*
> *institution in recorded history. I'm not saying that's ALL it*
> *has been responsible for. It has also been responsible for*
> *most of the great art and music of Western civilization. What's*

more, ANY institution that has exercised power and influence for a long time will have some skeletons in its closet, so it's only to be expected that the institution that has had the most influence for the longest time will have the most skeletons. There's nothing particularly startling about that. It's certainly not a slur on Catholics or the Catholic faith. Or a slur on your family. That would be utterly preposterous. Indeed, if anyone had suggested to me that your family couldn't grasp something as elemental as that, it would have made me angry. Because THAT would have been a gross insult to their intelligence. I have too much respect for their intelligence to believe for a moment that they can't distinguish between their role as Catholics and the Church's role in history. And anybody who says they can't is guilty of slander in my opinion.

Or you were only being yourself:

You know and I know—and I thought THEY knew—that I'm a crossword puzzle addict, so what could be more natural than sitting down after dinner and doing a crossword puzzle while the rest of you chatted? I wasn't being aloof. On the contrary, I can't think of a better way of showing them how comfortable and at home I feel around them. They ought to be flattered that I don't feel I have to dress up for them or try to impress them, that I can just be natural around them as I am around my own family.

Or you were only trying to be funny:

I really find it hard to believe that your mother took me seriously. She's always had such a wonderful sense of humor. Remember, SHE is the one who is always telling funny stories about your little sister's problems being the ugly duckling of the family. So naturally I thought she would think it funny when I suggested tying a piece of raw meat around your sister's neck so at least the dog would play with her. But I guess her sense of humor isn't what I thought it was. Either that or she's putting you on. Yes, I bet that's it. She's much too sophisticated to get upset about a joke like that.

Or you were only trying to pay a compliment:

I'm continually amazed at your brother's capacity for assuming that people are putting him down when in fact they're praising him. Look, when I called his old university a halfway house for mental defectives, designed to teach morons how to survive away from home without having to think, what I meant was that he owed his success to his own natural abilities and his appetite for hard work. In other words, all I was doing was giving HIM the credit for what he's achieved. HE deserves the credit, not the university. I wish he could see that. I want him to be proud of himself.

The special attractiveness of this particular type of excuse—*They took it the wrong way!*—lies not only in its proven effectiveness but also in what might be called its side-effectiveness. For it has the very beneficial side-effect of setting up an excellent all-purpose excuse for not visiting your in-laws:

Every time I go there I say or do something that annoys them. No matter how hard I try, they always find SOMETHING to get upset about. It's almost as if they make a point of misunderstanding me. Anyway, it's not worth it. It just makes everybody unhappy.

This excuse won't be valid forever, of course, but it's easily renewable. All you have to do, when you are finally dragooned into visiting your in-laws again, is start chatting merrily about Hitler's good points or the fun side of child-molesting and you can bet that you will be misunderstood all over again.

EXCUSES YOU SHOULD NEVER USE
FOR INSULTING THE IN-LAWS
. . . and the reasons why

I didn't know they could hear me.

So it's all right to insult them as long as you do it behind their backs?

Well, what I said happens to be true.

You call yourself an excuse-maker and yet you're willing to drag the truth into it?

Somebody had to tell them the facts of life.
Said who?

You never say anything when they insult ME.
No need to, if you're going to try to get even.

I apologized, didn't I?

That was your second mistake, apologizing, because it implied that your first mistake was something to apologize for. This excuse, then, is your third mistake.

. . . Disturbing the Neighbors

Just as in-laws were put on this earth to be insulted, so it is the sole function of neighbors to be disturbed. And like the insults that enrage your in-
laws, the disturbances that make your neighbors crazed are often ones that
could only be detected by someone pathologically committed to detecting
them. For instance, some years ago I received the following letter from the
gentleman in the apartment below mine:

> Dear Mr. Carroll,
>
> I very much regret having to complain, but we are frequently
> disturbed at a very early hour (5 A.M. this morning) and very late at
> night, by the indiscreet use of your toilets.
>
> The plumbing in this building is very poor and if not used dis-
> creetly the tenants below are always aware of the toilets being used,
> and this, coupled with flushing the toilets late at night or early
> morning, is most disturbing and also embarrassing.
>
> I am sorry that I have to draw your attention to this problem,
> but do so in the belief that you are unaware of the disturbance
> created. . . .

On first reading, I thought the letter merely hilarious: Some people become
deranged when they see a full moon at night, this man becomes deranged
when he hears a toilet flush at night. But on second reading I noticed that
the nocturnal flushing of the toilet was secondary to—not synonymous

with—the "indiscreet" use of the toilet. Clearly he had something else, something worse, on his mind. At length I was able to determine what it was: Not only had I been making my bladder gladder at all hours of the night, which was bad enough, but in doing so *I had been hitting the water*—a flagrant indiscretion that would have been audible to absolutely anyone who might happen to be standing on a ladder downstairs with his ear cupped to the ceiling.

My response to the letter, I'm sorry to say, bore few traces of my essentially gentle character. I forget the exact details—mercifully—but I remember that I proposed an alternative style of urinating which would have left his balcony, and indeed himself, glistening with unexpected moisture.

The moral of this story is twofold. First, you should be prepared (if you are not already) for the fact that however harmless and private and natural the activity in which you are engaged, there is probably someone nearby, a neighbor, going into paroxysms of disgust. Second, there is a difference between seriously disturbing your neighbors and having neighbors who are seriously disturbed. The latter, as exemplified by the gentleman who wrote me the above letter, may be dealt with any way you see fit. The former should be dealt with only through excuses.

The familial category is probably the best source of excuses because it has the greatest number of scapegoats:

> *You're right, the dog HAS been making a racket recently. And frankly I'm glad he has. That's why we got him. I don't know whether you were aware of it, but several of the neighbors have seen prowlers around here recently. And since my wife is alone a lot when I'm away on business, I thought it a good idea to get a dog. I WANT to hear barking whenever someone is wandering around the neighborhood* [or the building] *at night. Don't you?*

> *You heard loud music coming from HERE? Are you positive? Strange. It seems pretty quiet to me, but then I just got home. Maybe the kids were playing music and turned it off when they saw me coming. Anyway, I'll speak to them about it.*

Oh no, my son will be so depressed. You see, he had a childhood disease that left his right arm crippled, and as part of his therapy he's supposed to throw a ball for a certain period every day. The more accurate his throws get, the farther along he is in his rehabilitation. But if he's thrown the ball through your window AGAIN, he must still have a long way to go. You can't imagine what it's like having a handicapped child. When things like this happen I think maybe it would be better if I just sent him away somewhere.

You were only kept up HALF the night? In that case I'm moving in with you. I was kept up ALL night. My in-laws are staying with us, and the only way they know if they exist is to make noise. But they're supposed to leave tomorrow, so there's no point in investing in earplugs.

From the financial category:

Thanks for telling me. I mean that. The radio was SUPPOSED to be loud enough to be heard outside. I suppose you heard that we were burglarized last week, and since we can't afford an alarm system we thought we would discourage other would-be burglars and save money by leaving the radio turned up. Of course if we left it turned up TOO loud, like we have it now, that would also be a tip-off to burglars. So now we know to turn it down a bit. Thanks again.

And the medical:

You bet I know what time it is. If you have insomnia and an illuminated digital clock, you ALWAYS know what time it is. That's why I was doing my exercises—in hopes of tiring myself out so I could get to sleep. And it was working. Now, dammit, I'm wide awake again.

And the meteorological:

I can't understand it. We've always had the TV on at this hour and no one has ever complained. Oh, I know what it is. It's the weather. No, seriously. Today is one of those days between the heating season and the air-conditioning season when we have all the windows open. That must be why it bothered you.

And the technological:

It's the acoustics in this building. Somehow every sound is amplified and transmitted to the next apartment. In fact, we were only playing the music loud enough to drown out the music from upstairs. See what I mean?

And, lastly, the calendarial:

It IS noisy, isn't it? But I can't really do anything about it, not yet, because my husband threw a surprise birthday party for me and it would be rude of me to tell people to leave.

Helpful hints: If you are planning a major disturbance in the near future, start showing unaccustomed cordiality toward your neighbors. Wave to them in the street, hold doors open for them, pick up things they drop and run after them, steal their mail so that you can take it around to them yourself saying it was misdelivered, say extravagantly nice things about them to the neighborhood yenta, and so on. Then, as the time for your disturbance approaches, start letting them know that merrymaking on your premises impends, at the same time casually informing them that everyone else knows and no one objects. These precautionary measures will lessen the chances of a neighborhood-wide implosion when your debauch finally takes place.

Such tactics are unnecessary, and unavailing, with neighbors who are determined to be disturbed regardless. I'm talking about those tormented souls whom the gods forced to live within earshot of the squeaky mattress springs on which you disport or within telescopic range of the spot where you like to sunbathe in the nude. With these people all you can do is fall back on the sort of provocative drollery that later can be recycled as a dinner party anecdote:

So you're the person who lives below us. Well, I just want to thank you for all you've done for our marriage. Somehow the spark had gone out of it until we moved into this apartment, but then we found that the sound of your snoring was a fantastic turn-on. We consider ourselves very lucky to be living above you. Most people just make love in silence, or to the sound of music, but we make love to the sound of YOU. Sometimes at night we just sit around holding hands, waiting for those incredible nasal vibes that launch us on the road to ecstasy. The only problem is—and I hope you won't think this is a criticism—sometimes you finish before WE do. It's no big deal, really, and I shouldn't even mention it, but if you wouldn't mind, it would be really beautiful, I mean beautiful, if, you know, whenever you stop snoring prematurely you could just sort of, well, fake it for a little while longer. I know I'm being selfish, but otherwise we have to wait for those sexy thumps on your ceiling to get us going again.

Thank God, at last we can stop this boring business of lying around naked in the sun. At first we did it just because it was something to do. Then we did it because we found that every time we took off our clothes we saw these brilliant flashes, which we took to be a sign that our bodies were pleasurable in the sight of God. Then we did it because we realized that the brilliant flashes came from your binoculars, which we took to be a sure sign that we were giving YOU pleasure. And when we noticed that you never appeared at your window if we were dressed, we began to feel guilty. We felt we were disappointing you. We even considered buying you a subscription to Hustler *so you would have something to look at on cloudy days.*

Thus will you discover what it means to say something *pour épater le bourgeois.*

EXCUSES YOU SHOULD NEVER USE FOR
DISTURBING THE NEIGHBORS
. . . and the reasons why

It doesn't sound loud to me.
They guessed that already. That's why they're at the door.

I don't make a fuss when YOU have parties.
If you can't hear your own parties, how could you possibly hear theirs?

It's not MY fault if you go to bed early.
Actually, that's not quite what you're being blamed for.

I thought you were away for the weekend.
That's what you used to say when your parents came home unexpectedly and demanded to know what happened to all the Scotch.

This isn't a morgue, you know.
Don't give them ideas.

. . . *Failing to Answer a Letter*

The one nice thing about getting into trouble for failing to answer a letter is that the trouble is so easy to get out of. All you need is one of these guaranteed all-purpose excuses:

> *I never received it.*

> *But I DID answer it.*

Every other serviceable excuse is merely embroidery on these two basic designs. However, since most people show a marked inclination to believe embroidered excuses before plain ones, you would be wise to have on hand various explanations to stitch onto these all-purpose alibis.

For people who are puzzled as to why you never received their letter:

> *If you've been to a post office recently and have seen who they're hiring to handle the mail these days, you can't dismiss the possibility that they threw it in the trash when they couldn't find anyone who could read handwriting. Seriously, though, my guess is that the mailman put it in the wrong box downstairs. There's another person in the building with a name very similar to mine, and she's ALWAYS getting my mail. But normally she puts it out in the hall for me, so that I still get it within a day or so at most. The problem is she's on vacation at the moment, which means I have no way of finding out if your letter is in her box or not. I'd have to*

ambush the mailman—and I'm never here at that time of day. It's all very frustrating.

It's my own fault, or at least I SUSPECT it's my own fault. What happened was that we were planning to go away for the summer and so I sent a change-of-address notice to the local post office. Then when my wife become ill and we couldn't leave, I sent another notice rescinding the previous one. I even sent a notice to the post office in the other place asking them to send back any mail that was forwarded there. Well, you can't imagine the havoc this has created. Now I sit here virtually isolated from the outside world while the two post offices play Ping-Pong with my mail.

It's a complete mystery to me. All I know is that you're the fourth person this week to ask me about a letter I never received. I can't figure it out, because my BILLS don't seem to have any trouble in reaching me. And my junk mail still arrives as regularly as clockwork. You know, if I were paranoid I think I'd begin to wonder if maybe my mail was being intercepted. I don't think I'm paranoid, but STILL I'm beginning to wonder. I know what I'll do. I'll send myself a letter, and if it doesn't get through I'll know something funny is going on.

For people who are puzzled as to why they never received your answer:

I can't understand why you haven't got it by now. I must have mailed it, let's see, five . . . no, six days ago. On the other hand, I'm not exactly shocked. Yesterday I received two letters—this is absolutely true—one of which was mailed on the 13th in London and the other on the 9th on the other side of town! It would have gotten here sooner if they had put it between their teeth and crawled here with it. Anyway, wait another couple of days and if it hasn't arrived by then give me a call. In the meantime I'll see if I can find the carbon.

That's strange. I remember writing it, and I distinctly remember giving it to my cleaning lady to mail—because I'd run out of stamps and wanted her to pick some up at the post office for me at the same time. Oh Christ, you don't suppose she mailed it without a stamp, do you? I didn't think to check and see how many stamps she came back with.

I know very well why you didn't receive it. Because I'm looking at it right now. It came back today with a bit of graffiti on it that reads "Not At This Address." And when I looked at the address I realized that, sure enough, they were right. You're NOT at 2724 Glyndon Avenue. You're at 2427 Glyndon Avenue, aren't you? Unless of course this is YOUR handwriting, ha ha. Actually, now that I look at it more closely . . .

Anyway, so long as you remember that you never received their letter but that you did answer it, you will either have two perfect excuses or the worst single excuse ever invented by an adult.

EXCUSES YOU SHOULD NEVER USE FOR
FAILING TO ANSWER A LETTER
. . . and the reasons why

Things have been so hectic recently.
St. Paul's life was pretty hectic too, but he still found the time to write the odd epistle.

I didn't know you wanted a WRITTEN reply.
What did you think they wanted? Smoke signals?

I was going to take it in and put it with the office mail, but I'm so forgetful.
And cheap.

I haven't been feeling well lately.
You had writer's cramp?

You know how bad I am about answering letters.
Now they do, and it doesn't help.

. . . Failing to Return a Telephone Call

The telephone, that great boon to all makers of excuses, can become the bane of your existence when the instrument itself is the focus of the excuse. Unlike the postal service, where your communications are consigned to faceless intermediaries, the telephone system involves direct contact. What's more, if for any reason the system fails to work, which is highly unlikely, you are immediately aware of it and can avail yourself of an alternative telephone. Consequently, the force behind the two classic excuses for failing to answer a letter—i.e., sabotaged by a gremlin or gremlins unknown—cannot be cited for failure to return a call.

Nonetheless, the same excuses for not answering a letter provide useful models for the two basic excuses you will need for failing to return a call:

> *I never got your message.*

> *But I TRIED to call back.*

When elaborating on the first excuse, you can choose from these explanations:

> *What message? Whom did you speak to? Jesus, this is ridiculous. That's the third message this week she's forgotten to give me—or the third message I KNOW about. God knows how many others fell down that hole at the bottom of her brain. Look, will you do me a favor? In future make sure she*

writes down the message while you're still on the phone. That will at least shorten the odds against the message ever reaching me.

Oh, YOU were the one who called! I was in the shower when he gave me the message, and I thought he said "Call Alan." Which struck me as a bit odd, because I know only one Alan and I haven't spoken to him in over a year. But I called him anyway, and when HE didn't know anything about it I really became confused. Well, that's today's mystery cleared up. So how are you, Ellen?

Yes, she did leave a message for me—but she left it on the refrigerator where she keeps her shopping list and I didn't see it until I went to get some ice for my drink. By then, of course, you'd already left the office. Hey, maybe you've just given me a good reason to start drinking earlier in the day. . . .

I was supposed to call YOU back? I thought he said you were going to call ME back. In fact, I know that's what he said. He never listens to a word that's said to him. As a result I end up waiting around all day for you to call me back. That dunce.

Elaborations for the second basic excuse include:

Ah, THERE you are! I was beginning to think you had skipped town. I've been calling you for days. . . . Really? That's very strange. One thing I know for certain: SOMEBODY isn't home, because somebody hasn't been answering their phone for days. I don't see how I could have been calling the wrong number because I know your number backwards. Then again, maybe that's the problem. Maybe I've been DIALING it backwards. Is there such a thing as numerical dyslexia? Probably not. Oh well.

The reason I haven't gotten back to you is that someone keeps getting back to ME. A heavy breather, would you believe! Actually, he's more asthmatic than heavy, but it's not the breathing that's the problem; it's the fact that he never hangs up, even after I do. So my line stays tied up. I've called the phone company, the police, everyone, but all they can do is find out the number he's calling from—it's always a public phone—and then sever the connection. If it keeps up I guess I'll have to have my number changed. Anyway, that's the story of me and my telephone. How about you?

I got your message and I called back right away. And I got this recording that said your phone had been disconnected. Honestly. I phoned back several times just to make sure, and each time I got the same recording: "The number you have dialed, 5-8-0-7-9-8-1, is no longer . . ." What? 7891? Oh. Well, no wonder. . . .

I tried to call you back but my phone wasn't working. And you know WHY it wasn't working? This is the good part. Shortly after you called, my husband got into a shouting match with his mother over the telephone. And after he hung up he unplugged the phone so that she couldn't phone back and get in her famous Last Word. Then he went out and forgot to plug the phone back in again, so that when I came home and saw that you had called, the line was dead. Finally, after I'd already arranged for the phone company to send somebody out, he came home and realized immediately what the problem was. But he did have the good grace to be embarrassed about it.

And should you get yourself into a situation where messages to call a particular person have begun to pile up like autumn leaves, depriving you of most of the good excuses for not calling back, the solution is to go ahead and call him back—at all the wrong times. It's not that difficult, you know, to plot the trajectory of your calls so that they arrive just after he's left for work, or for lunch, or for home. And, of course, when you are asked if you want to leave a message for him, you sigh the sigh of the terminally exasperated, and after a weary pause you say:

Yes. Could you just ask him to call me back?

EXCUSES YOU SHOULD NEVER USE
FOR FAILING TO RETURN
A TELEPHONE CALL
. . . and the reasons why

I was just about to call you.
If you know anyone who would believe this, you move in the wrong circles.

I assumed you had gone away for the weekend.
They didn't ask you to assume, they asked you to call.

I called but your line was busy.
That means you knew they were home, but still you didn't bother to try again.

I had to go out of town.
You went someplace where they don't have telephones?

I couldn't call. I had a crowd of people here.
And they wrestled you to the ground every time you reached for the telephone, right?

. . . Failing to Return Hospitality

As is so often the case, the best possible reason for failing to return hospitality makes for an appallingly incendiary excuse:

> *Once was enough.*

Nor will you find favor with your friends if you dwell on the perils of back-and-forth entertaining, especially that of becoming benumbed by one another's company but not wishing to violate the unspoken concordat by which you troop to each other's doorstep at every phase of the moon.

So to preserve amity you will have to swathe in a veil of excuses your lack of enthusiasm for reciprocal entertaining. Conveniently, these excuses are distributed more or less equally among the various categories.

From the familial category:

> *Tell me, what's it like having the run of your own house? I used to have similar privileges in MY house, but it's been so long that I've forgotten what it's like. Ever since my brother-in-law came to stay with us I've felt like I'm just a boarder here. I can't even have friends over for coffee without him butting in. I wouldn't dream of trying to do any REAL entertaining with him here. And it looks like he's going to be around for some time to come. Originally he was just going to stay a couple of weeks while he looked for a place to live. But I think he's decided that he likes the rent-free life, and my husband refuses to throw him out. It's a dreadful nuisance, really.*

From the financial:

You don't know how I envy you being able to afford little luxuries like a table to eat on. Somehow, when we were furnishing the apartment, we managed to run out of money between the sofa and the table and chairs, so now we sit comfortably on the sofa and fantasize about the day when we can invite people over for something more interesting than just standing around.

The medical:

If I sound cross, it's because I am. I've had it up to here with our maid. It seems like she's always sick when we need her most. To be fair, she isn't in very good health, but it does seem as if she times her illnesses so that they come at the worst possible moment. It's got to the point where we can't plan more than a day ahead, if that, and of course entertaining is out of the question. I don't want to have to get rid of her, but I don't want to go the rest of my life without being able to have friends over for dinner.

The meteorological:

I don't know how I'm going to survive until the warm weather gets here. The only cooking we ever do is on the barbecue, which means that we have months of restaurants and sandwiches to look forward to. Not that I mind, it's just that one's friends aren't particularly enthralled by the idea of coming over for a sandwich.

The technological:

We'd love to be able to put you up when you come to town, but our apartment is roughly the size of the average pantry. And even that may be an aspersion on the average pantry. I'm not joking. We bounce off the walls like two moths inside a lampshade. So unless you know how to sleep standing up . . .

The calendarial:

> *I wish you people would reorganize your lives. You KNOW*
> *the only time we have free for entertaining is on the*
> *weekends, yet you stick to your antisocial timetable. It would*
> *be so much fun to have you over, but how CAN we when you*
> *insist on vanishing every Friday?*

Whichever type of excuse you decide best suits your purposes, you would do well to remember that getting into trouble with friends for not returning hospitality is like getting into trouble with a submarine: The first confirmation you have that you are indeed in trouble is a quick flash of torpedo just beneath the surface of your relationship, by which time it is too late to do much about it.

It is therefore imperative that you get your excuse in as early as possible—preferably while you are enjoying the hospitality that you have no intention of repaying. It is fatal to wait until it dawns on your friends that they only ever see you *chez eux.* Likewise, it is important that your excuse be valid for an indefinite period of time. If it is one of those excuses that has an expiration date—a bad cold, a business trip—you will only succeed in postponing the trouble.

And whenever you begin to weary of dodging the torpedo, you can always throw yourself into reverse and issue a sudden invitation—very sudden, at the shortest possible notice. If this doesn't work—if, that is, there appears to be a danger that they will accept despite the short notice—you quickly add that you're inviting them to come and eat soul food and listen to your niece read her new epic poem about Botswana's struggle for independence.

And if *that* doesn't work, well, your niece will just have to have a terrible accident.

EXCUSES YOU SHOULD NEVER USE FOR
FAILING TO RETURN HOSPITALITY
. . . and the reasons why

I thought you didn't like parties.
They don't. It's invitations they like.

We've decided not to do any more entertaining for a while.
Any *more* entertaining? You've been entertaining *other* people?

I didn't want to bother you when you were going through such a difficult time.
Very thoughtful of you. People love being neglected when they're going through a difficult time.

It's a pity you live so far away.
They're closer than you think.

You would have been bored.
Perhaps, but it beats being excluded.

. . . Being Caught in a Compromising Situation

There are, of course, many compromising situations in which you may find yourself—or, more to the point, in which others may find you—but we all know that there is only one real *Compromising Situation*.

There are many situations in which prudence would seem to dictate a swift departure, but there is only one in which grown men have been known to leap out of windows stark naked in the middle of winter. And there are many situations in which your mate might want to strangle you, but there is only one in which a homicide jury might decide that strangling was too good for you.

That situation, obviously, is the one in which you are discovered in the arms, or worse, of someone to whom you are not wed, or betrothed, or otherwise committed—by someone to whom you are. Not a comfortable situation to be in. In fact, as situations go, this is about as uncomfortable as they get.

Considering, then, that this situation represents the supreme test of your skill as an excuse-maker, it may come as a surprise to you to learn that the most effective excuse you can make is simply an adult version of a childhood classic. Thus, whenever you have the misfortune to be caught in an unauthorized embrace, you say essentially the same thing you used to say when you were caught in the bathroom with the little boy or girl next door:

I was only playing doctor.

That is to say, you were only conducting a therapeutic exercise. It had nothing whatever to do with base desires on your part. It was entirely for the benefit of (1) the person you were caught with, or (2) the person who caught you.

Your explanation of the first therapy method will go something like this:

> *He was so depressed and so pitiful that I felt sorry for him. I was really frightened that he was right on the edge. All he could talk about was how old he was getting, how lonely he was, how ugly he was. What was especially sad was the way he went on about how he had always wanted to be like you—handsome, sexy, attractive to women—and how his spirit had been shattered when he finally admitted to himself that he'd never be able to measure up to you. So I thought it was the least I could do to try to give him a little confidence in himself, to make him think that maybe he IS attractive to women. Of course the awful truth is that he's not in the least attractive—certainly compared to YOU—and he's so pathetically unsure of himself that it's an ordeal to try to be intimate with him. But I knew that beforehand. The only reason I went through with it was that I thought it might help him feel better about himself—and I knew you would understand. I knew you were too compassionate and too strong to feel jealous or threatened the way an unfeeling, weak little man would.*

A variation:

> *It was an act of mercy, pure and simple. He's dying. But that's only part of it. You see, we had an affair many years ago—long before I met you—which I ended because I knew it would never come to anything. Frankly, I just wasn't that turned on by him. But when he came around and told me that he had this terminal illness, and that it would mean so much to him if, you know, we could do it one last time, I thought it would be cruel to say no. It would have been like refusing a condemned man's last request. So I asked myself what YOU would have done in that situation, and then I knew I was doing the right thing.*

With the second type of therapy, the one undertaken exclusively to benefit the person who caught you in the middle of your therapeutic writhings, you will want to fashion an excuse along the following lines:

> *What do you mean she was your best friend? She IS your best friend. She just proved it. Don't you realize that she only did that for YOU? Look, we both know that I'm not able to satisfy you in bed, not the way you would like, and that breaks my heart, because I want nothing more than for you to be fulfilled. So I finally got up the courage to ask her if she would be willing to act as a surrogate—like the ones you read about in those sex-counseling clinics—in the hope that maybe I could learn how to give you pleasure. And I thought it was beginning to work. Wasn't it? Hasn't it been better for you lately? Please say it has. Please say it was worth all the pain she's gone through for you—the pain of knowing that she was just being used as a vehicle for me to give YOU pleasure, and then the pain of having you burst in like that and make such a scene and say all those hurtful things. After that, I wouldn't blame her if she never forgives you.*

Or, as a more aggressive alternative:

> *If you would shut up and THINK for a minute you would realize that I was only trying to find a cure for your headaches. After all, when is the only time you complain of having a headache? When I express some form of erotic interest, right? And you haven't complained of a headache in over a month, right? So why are you complaining about not having a headache to complain about? You can't have it both ways, you know. Either I give you a headache, or I give HER one. And since I'm married to you and not her, I thought it only right that she should be the one to get the headache. But if you disagree, we can talk about it while I fondle your breasts.*

A mite *too* brazen, you say? Wrong. Regardless of whether you're a spare-time psychoanalyst or an amateur gynecologist, no one has the right to invade your consulting room and interfere with the treatment of your patients. Playing doctor is a serious business.

As the late Dr. Henry Miller once said, after he had walked out on a wife who had slyly and successfully schemed to catch him *in flagrante,* "I couldn't tolerate being married to a woman who didn't trust me."

EXCUSES YOU SHOULD NEVER USE FOR BEING CAUGHT IN A COMPROMISING SITUATION
. . and the reasons why

Can I help it if she went crazy for my body?
Apparently. You've somehow managed to put off everyone else who was ever tempted to go crazy for your body.

He took advantage of me.
People usually *do* take what they're offered.

I didn't know what I was doing.
If you're believed, you have more problems than you thought you had.

I did nothing to encourage her.
Cheap floozies don't need encouraging. That's why they go for people like you.

You knew what I was like when you married me.
No, *then* it was only an ugly rumor.

. . . Being Caught Making a Poor Excuse

We have now reached a conundrum: If, as I have endeavored to show, there is a good excuse for everything, it follows that there should be no excuse for making a poor excuse. On the other hand, it also follows that there should be a good excuse even for that.

There is. It comes in three forms, depending on whether you blame the prior excuse on your thoughtfulness, your laziness, or your silliness. If you were just being thoughtful, your covering excuse will take this shape:

> *It was stupid of me, I know, to think you wouldn't see through that excuse, but I was trying not to hurt you, that's all. I figured it didn't much matter WHAT I said, since it wouldn't make any difference to the situation. So given a choice between saying something harmless and saying something that might upset you, I chose harmless. Of course, I chose wrong.*

Or if you were being lazy:

> *I hate to admit it, but the real reason was so bizarre, and so unbelievably complicated, that I decided it wasn't worth going into. I felt it would be easier just to make up a simple excuse. Which I did. Unfortunately, I also made it simple-minded, and naturally you saw through it.*

Or, finally, if you were being silly:

I was only kidding. I can't believe you took me seriously. You know where I got that excuse from, don't you? It comes from The Best Excuse. *It's one of the excuses that the author says you should never use. And how right he was! By the way, if you don't have the book, you must get it. It's wonderful. Not only has it changed my life, but . . .*

That will do fine. Thank you.

EXCUSES YOU SHOULD NEVER USE FOR
BEING CAUGHT MAKING A POOR EXCUSE
. . . and the reasons why

I was just trying to get your attention.
Twit, that's the last thing you want to get.

What difference does it make? You wouldn't have believed me anyway.
They must know you quite well.

You just have a suspicious nature.
They *do* know you quite well.

You believed me the last time.
Whatever the excuse was, you can retire it now for good.

I don't understand. Donald Carroll recommended it.
Please, say anything but this.

APPENDIX I

One Hundred and One Useful Phobias
for the Making of Excuses

FEAR OF .	MEDICAL TERM
people	anthropophobia
men	androphobia
women	gynophobia
virgins	parthenophobia
crowds	demophobia
bad men	scelerophobia
robbers	harpaxophobia
blacks	negrophobia
whites	caucasophobia
foreigners	xenophobia
ghosts	phantasmophobia
self	autophobia

* * * * * * * * * * * * * * * * * * *

animals	zoophobia
insects	entomophobia
birds	ornithophobia
bees	apiphobia
cats	ailurophobia
dogs	cynophobia
fish	icthyophobia
frogs	batrachophobia
snakes	ophidiophobia
spiders	arachneophobia
tapeworms	taeniophobia

FEAR OF . . .	MEDICAL TERM
many things	polyphobia
places	topophobia
large objects	megalophobia
small objects	microphobia
high objects	batophobia
houses	domatophobia
ladders	klimakophobia
streets	agyiophobia
bridges	gephyrophobia
vehicles	amaxophobia
trains	siderodromophobia
machinery	mechanophobia
metal	metallophobia
knives	aichmophobia
glass	crystallophobia
mirrors	spectrophobia
fire	pyrophobia
water	hydrophobia
anything new	kainophobia

* * * * * * * * * * * * * * * * * *

functioning	ergasiophobia
eating	pagophobia
thinking	phronemophobia
sitting down	kathisophobia
standing up	stasiphobia
walking	basiphobia
crossing streets	dromophobia
school	school phobia
work	ponophobia
sleep	hypnophobia
travel	hodophobia
being enclosed	claustrophobia
being looked at	scopophobia
writing	graphophobia

FEAR OF . . .	MEDICAL TERM
speaking	laliophobia
hearing certain words	onomatophobia
failure	kakorrhaphiophobia

* * * * * * * * * * * * * * * * *

sex	genophobia
being touched	haphephobia
naked body	gymnophobia
female genitals	eurotophobia
hair	trichopathophobia
rectum	proctophobia
sexual intercourse	coitophobia
semen	spermatophobia
syphilis	syphilophobia
venereal disease	cypridophobia
marriage	gamophobia
jealousy	zelophobia
sinning	peccatiphobia
pleasure	hedonophobia

* * * * * * * * * * * * * * * * *

ideas	ideophobia
time	chronophobia
motion	kinesophobia
stillness	eremiophobia
daylight	phengophobia
darkness	nyctophobia
dawn	eosophobia
sounds	acousticophobia
color	chromatophobia
air	aerophobia
height	acrophobia
depth	bathophobia
left	levophobia
right	dextrophobia
materialism	hylephobia

FEAR OF . . .	MEDICAL TERM
money	chrematophobia
poverty	peniaphobia
ruin	atephobia
responsibility	hypengyophobia
weakness	asthenophobia
disease	pathophobia
medicine	pharmacophobia
emptiness	kenophobia
change	neophobia
electricity	electrophobia
gravity	barophobia
infinity	apeirophobia

* * * * * * * * * * * * * * * * * *

everything	panphobia

APPENDIX II

One Dozen Excuses
to Be Avoided at All Times

For the following wretched excuses I am indebted to the late Admiral Hyman Rickover, a man not best known for suffering fools gladly. Admiral Rickover kept these excuses posted on his office door along with a note requesting members of his staff to make their excuses simply by referring to the appropriate numbers:

1. I thought I told you.
2. That's the way we've always done it.
3. No one told me to go ahead.
4. I didn't think it was that important.
5. I'm so busy I just couldn't get around to it.
6. Why bother? The Admiral won't buy it.
7. I didn't know you were in a hurry for it.
8. That's *his* job, not mine.
9. I forgot.
10. I'm waiting for the OK.
11. That's not my department.
12. How was I to know this was different?